WITH SCOTT TO THE POLE
The *Terra Nova* Expedition 1910–1913

WITH SCOTT TO THE POLE

The *Terra Nova* Expedition 1910–1913

The Photographs of Herbert Ponting

TED SMART

First published in Great Britain 2004
Bloomsbury Publishing Plc, 38 Soho Square, London W1D 3HB

This edition produced for the Book People Ltd 2004
Hall Wood Avenue
Haydock
St Helens WA11 9UL

A CIP catalogue record for this book is available from the British Library

Published by arrangement with Book Creation Ltd., London, and Book
Creation LLC, New York
Publishing Directors: Hal Robinson and John Kelly

Photography permissions:
© Photographs by Herbert Ponting reproduced under license from the
Royal Geographical Society, London, unless otherwise stated in the picture
acknowledgments on page 240. All rights reserved.

© Photographs from the Bowers album and Herbert Ponting's panoramas
reproduced by permission of Scott Polar Research Institute, University
of Cambridge, as noted in the picture acknowledgments on page 240.
All rights reserved.

All other photographs are listed in the picture acknowledgments on page 240.

Dates listed underneath the captions in the portfolio and gallery sections are a
guide to when the photograph was taken. In some cases, where the precise
day is not known, the month or year alone is provided.

Contributors and consultants:
H. J. P ("Douglas") Arnold, Dr Liz Cruwys, Professor Julian Dowdeswell,
Sir Ranulph Fiennes, and Dr Beau Riffenburgh

Special thanks to Professor Julian Dowdeswell for all his help and advice in
the preparation of this book.

Designer: Peter Laws
Managing Editor: Tamiko Rex
Copy Editors: Jonathan Dore and Janice Anderson

Photographs on pages:
2. The Matterhorn Berg and Mt. Erebus (Clissold on summit)
3. Herbert Ponting and telephoto apparatus
5. Mt. Erebus and ice reflection in foreground

Front cover: Western Party crossing the ice to the *Terra Nova*
Back cover: Scott's Polar Party at the South Pole
Jacket flap photograph (back): Herbert Ponting and telephoto apparatus
Spine photograph: Steward Hooper eating baked beans on a wooden box
advertising Heinz

Printed and bound in Singapore

ISBN 0-7475-7650-5

10 9 8 7 6 5 4 3 2 1

CONTENTS

FOREWORD

SIR RANULPH FIENNES

FOR CENTURIES, JOURNEYS INTO THE UNKNOWN by explorers, merchants, scientists such as Darwin on the *Beagle*, or hunters such as those on the polar whaling fleets, told terrifying tales and sketched imaginative drawings to depict what they had seen, often with a good deal of artistic license.

The Antarctic wanderings of Captain James Cook in the 1750s and James Clark Ross in the 1830s were described in magazines and books with lurid illustrations of huge curling waves and towering icebergs, ever-poised above the tiny but heroic ships of the venturers.

Some seventy years later, when Britain first sent Torpedo Lieutenant Captain Robert Falcon Scott and his ship *Discovery* south to Antarctica, the box camera had been invented and was as vital a part of any expedition as a pith helmet or an ice axe. That was in 1901—the 20th century—yet Antarctica was still unexplored. Nobody even knew if it was a continent or merely a mass of floating ice. In 1910, Scott's *Terra Nova* expedition was sent to penetrate this vast and hostile region, to devise the best method of travel there, and, with a band of top-rate scientists under his control, to gain knowledge in the cause of science. He chose the best scientists from all over the Commonwealth as well as the best professional photographer-cum-cinematographer, Herbert Ponting, whose reputation was already firmly established in London after an exciting life in remote lands about which he lectured with magic lantern slides.

This book confirms Ponting was one of the truly great photographers of the 20th century, especially considering the extremely demanding conditions under which he had to work in Antarctica. In the 1970s, I worked as a photographer and cinematographer in Antarctica and even then, with vastly improved cameras, lenses, films, and ancillary gear, I still found even the simplest photographic activity extremely demanding in the ultra-low temperatures.

In the 1970s, a character-assassinating biography of Scott and a nine-hour equally distorted television program based upon that book attacked the explorer and his achievements. His posthumous record was besmirched and, in 2002, I decided to set the record straight and reassert historical reality in place of the groundless myths successfully propagated by the book and the film. I am delighted that my resulting book *Captain Scott* is now followed by this brilliantly produced Royal Geographical Society and Scott Polar Research Institute publication, which shows the stark reality of the conditions faced by Scott and his men, the very first human beings to penetrate and learn about Antarctica.

Scott, Shackleton, and Amundsen were all brilliant polar travelers. All of the men made serious errors, but all achieved major successes. Amundsen was the first to reach the Pole, towed there by dog power; Scott was the first to arrive by pure man power. The US scientific station at the South Pole is called the Scott Amundsen South Pole Station in recognition of two great but very different achievements.

The greatest of French polar explorers, Dr. Jean Charcot, wrote in *Le Matin* (and remember that Frenchmen are not, by nature, inclined to be Anglophiles): "Scott has conquered the Pole. The public, ill-informed, will say that he reached his goal only second: but those who know—Amundsen and Shackleton among them—will say that it was Scott who opened the road to the Pole and mapped out the route, shedding a reflecting glow upon his country." He added: "Scott did not turn aside from his scientific program … It is quite another thing with Amundsen. He is not a scientist. He is bent only on setting up a record. If one wishes to pronounce the one greater than the other, the preference must go to him who surrounds his expedition result with the greatest number of discoveries and scientific observations."

One of Amundsen's great Pole team members, Helmer Hanssen, said: "It is no disparagement of Amundsen and the rest of us when I say that Scott's achievement far exceeded ours … Just imagine what it meant for Scott and the others to drag their sleds themselves, with all their equipment and provisions to the Pole. We started with 52 dogs and came back with 11, and many of these wore themselves out on the journey. What shall we say of Scott and his comrades, who were their own dogs? Anyone with any experience will take off his hat to Scott's achievement. I do not believe men ever have shown such endurance at any time, nor do I believe there ever will be men to equal it."

This book is a fitting tribute not only to Herbert Ponting, an artist of the highest quality, but also to a story of great heroism and courage.

Sir Ranulph Fiennes

The Road to the Pole

BEAU RIFFENBURGH AND LIZ CRUWYS

THE ROAD TO THE POLE

BEAU RIFFENBURGH AND LIZ CRUWYS

A CENTURY AGO THE ANTARCTIC REMAINED SHROUDED in mystery. It was seen as the last of nature's great secrets, the final blank, white space on the map. No one knew what the perpetual ice, the frigid temperatures, and the gale-force winds protected in the interior of this vast land mass that was larger than Europe or Australia. Was it covered by a giant icecap like that in Greenland? Was there simply an endless array of jagged peaks as in Norway's Svalbard within the Arctic Circle? Or did it consist primarily of an immense, low-lying barrier of ice that joined countless islands in a vast archipelago?

In the 1810s and 1820s commercial expeditions hunting for seals had explored much of the sub-Antarctic, concentrating on the region surrounding the South Shetland Islands, the tip of the Antarctic Peninsula, and the Weddell Sea. Then, during the following two decades, three major national expeditions—one British, one French, and one American—investigated and charted widely separated sections of coastline, helping to define the boundaries of what they thought might be a southern continent.

Of the three, the most successful was the British expedition from 1839 to 1843, which was under the command of Sir James Clark Ross. Sailing in HMS *Erebus* and *Terror*, Ross circumnavigated the continent and, south of New Zealand, became the first to force a way through the pack ice into the huge sea that now bears his name. Ross charted roughly 485 nautical miles (900 km) of new coastline in what he named Victoria Land before sighting an island on which stood two volcanoes that he named for his ships. (The nautical mile, equal to one-sixtieth of a degree of latitude or 1.852 km, was used by the naval explorers of Antarctica and is the mile unit used throughout this book.) Ross then discovered one of the Earth's most amazing geographical features, the vast expanse of ice—larger than Spain—that came to be known as the Great Ice Barrier and that today is named the Ross Ice Shelf.

Ross also managed to establish a new record for the farthest south yet reached, 78° 10' S, surpassing the 74° 15' S achieved by James Weddell some 20 years earlier. Strangely, despite these accomplishments, serious exploration of the Antarctic ground to a halt following Ross's expedition. For the next half century, the Antarctic slipped out of the public consciousness, and explorers, geographical societies, and governments turned their attention to opening up the great blank spaces on the maps of central Africa and the Arctic.

The return of Antarctic exploration to the international geographical agenda was, to a great extent, due to the long, lonely efforts of two men: the German scientist Georg von Neumayer and the British geographer Clements Markham. During the 1880s, each had independently, and unsuccessfully, argued for the benefits that could accrue if expeditions were sent to the far south of the globe. Then in 1893 Markham's power base grew considerably stronger when he became president of the Royal Geographical Society (RGS) in England. He immediately launched a new campaign for the revival of British Antarctic exploration, enlisting the aid of John Murray, Britain's foremost academic authority on the polar regions, in the matter.

Murray and Markham made impassioned pleas for British scientific societies to back an expedition to the Antarctic to answer questions of meteorology, geology, and terrestrial magnetism, as well as to add to basic geographical knowledge. They also stressed that the research then being carried out on two Antarctic whaling expeditions was demonstrating the value Antarctic science might have on human understanding of the natural world.

Their persistent efforts to galvanize interest in Antarctic exploration were met with overwhelming support in 1895 at the Sixth International Geographical Congress in London. A resolution was passed stating that "the exploration of the Antarctic Regions is the greatest piece of geographical exploration still to be undertaken. That, in view of the additions to knowledge in almost every branch of science which would result from such a scientific exploration, the Congress recommends that the scientific societies throughout the world should urge, in whatever way seems to them most effective, that this work should be undertaken before the close of the century."

The Congress also advocated extensive cooperation between Markham's proposed British expedition and Neumayer's German one. The two men soon divided the Antarctic into four quadrants, assigning two to the British and two to the Germans. Both then began afresh their attempts to launch national expeditions to the region.

Before either was successful in obtaining official backing, however, they were beaten off the mark by a Belgian expedition under the command of Adrien de Gerlache. This sailed in August 1897 in the ship *Belgica*, with an international crew that included a Norwegian mate (Roald Amundsen), an American surgeon (Frederick A. Cook), and a Polish geologist (Henryk Arçtowski). All three men were to make indelible marks in the world of polar exploration and science. After visiting Tierra del Fuego and the South Shetland Islands, de Gerlache took his ship along the eastern side of the Antarctic Peninsula, where they discovered and mapped new islands and waterways before being beset in the ice. Unable to escape and confined to their ship, they became the first people ever to winter south of the Antarctic Circle, before finally breaking free in 1899 after 13 months locked in the ice.

Meanwhile another expedition was also underway—and it was one that was particularly galling to Markham, who was having difficulty raising funds for his expedition. This new expedition was led by Carsten Borchgrevink, an Anglo-Norwegian who several years earlier had claimed to be the first person to set foot on the Antarctic continent. Then, Borchgrevink had been a member of an expedition sent to determine whether there were enough whales in the Southern Ocean to support an Antarctic whaling industry. When a party landed at Cape Adare in Victoria Land (the coast that Ross had charted), Borchgrevink jumped out of the boat first. Although his claim to priority was inaccurate—the American sealer John Davis had landed on the Antarctic Peninsula as early as 1821— for the moment it gave him a certain amount of celebrity. Upon his return to Britain, he used this in an attempt to raise money for an expedition of his own.

After a couple of years of unproductive petitioning, Borchgrevink suddenly received from one source all of the funding he needed. The press baron George Newnes contributed £40,000, allowing Borchgrevink to purchase and outfit a ship that he renamed *Southern Cross*. With a crew primarily consisting of Norwegians—even though the

Southern Cross in the pack ice. Having first encountered the pack far north of where they expected it to be on December 30, 1898, the men of Borchgrevink's expedition were not finally through it until mid-February 1899. It then took them 12 days to unload all the materials required for the first wintering ever on the Antarctic continent.

expedition was officially British—they sailed south in August 1898. They landed at Cape Adare, where two prefabricated huts were assembled and a party of 10 was left to winter. This was the first scientific party ever to do so on the Antarctic continent itself.

During the next year, despite having inadvertently chosen one of the most exposed and harshest parts of the Antarctic coast, the party obtained extensive scientific data. However, their winter consisted of near misses with disaster and bitter feuds between Borchgrevink, who was far from a natural leader, and his scientific staff. When the spring came, the party was picked up and the men continued their investigation of the Ross Sea region. They found that the Great Ice Barrier had receded some 30 miles (56 km) since Ross's expedition, and on February 16, 1899, near what would become known as the Bay of Whales, the entire party disembarked to have their photograph taken at the farthest south ever reached by a ship. The next day Borchgrevink and two companions sledged over a featureless landscape for approximately 10 miles (18 km), reaching a new farthest south of 78° 50'.

Despite his record and the completion of a detailed scientific program, Borchgrevink's expedition was to a great extent ignored. His lack of leadership skills and his too-obvious efforts at personal aggrandizement overshadowed the expedition's accomplishments, as did his faulty handling of many of the scientific materials and records kept by his colleagues. Even more important, however, he returned to Britain at a time when attention was being given instead to the preparations for another expedition. Clements Markham was finally nearing his goal.

Scott's British National Antarctic Expedition, 1901–04

In March 1899, the prospects for Markham's expedition had dramatically changed when Llewellyn Longstaff, a successful businessman and long-term fellow of the RGS, offered £25,000 to launch the project. Quickly thereafter the RGS and the Royal Society, which had joined forces in the venture, began developing plans for a purpose-built ship for the expedition. During the summer the government offered to donate £45,000 to the expedition on the condition that this sum should be matched by private subscriptions. With such backing, the additional monies were not long in coming—the British National Antarctic Expedition had been born.

The flag at Cape Adare with the two Lapps who accompanied Carsten Borchgrevink's expedition, easily identifiable by their distinctive head gear. Borchgrevink named the base Camp Ridley in honor of his mother. He did not know that he had selected a particularly inhospitable part of the coast for his wintering.

Securing the finances for the expedition did not end all problems, however. The ensuing months would prove that the goals and plans of the RGS and the Royal Society were decidedly different. The representatives of the RGS held the view that geographical discovery was the primary objective of the expedition, while those from the Royal Society—Britain's most prestigious scientific organization—felt its purpose was to engage in scientific research. This ultimately led to a dispute over who should lead the expedition. The Royal Society wished to have the noted scientist John W. Gregory in charge, thereby following the same pattern of leadership as three other Antarctic projects that were then in preparation: the German expedition under Erich von Drygalski, a Swedish effort under Otto Nordenskjöld, and the Scottish research expedition under William Speirs Bruce.

Markham, however, had other ideas. He wanted the entire operation to emphasize geographical exploration rather than science and to be conducted under the auspices of the Royal Navy, in which he had spent his formative years. His choice as commander was the torpedo lieutenant of HMS *Majestic*, Robert Falcon Scott. Scott had first come to Markham's attention in 1887, when, as a midshipman, he had won a sailing race that Markham had been watching. Scott had neither the polar experience nor the scientific training of Gregory, but he was Markham's candidate, and Markham was an inveterate intriguer of championship caliber. With the help of another backroom powerbroker, Sir George Goldie, Markham ultimately forced his will upon the Royal Society, and Gregory resigned. With Gregory's departure the expedition became what Markham wanted: a voyage of geographical discovery in which science was subordinated to naval adventure.

Markham's influence went further than mere politicking for expedition leaders, however, and it would be felt in British exploration throughout the next decade. In the 1850s he had participated in one of the naval expeditions sent out in search of Sir John Franklin in the North American Arctic (Franklin and his two ships—coincidentally HMS *Erebus* and *Terror*—had disappeared in 1845), and this had shaped his beliefs regarding how a polar expedition should be conducted. Half a century later, he saw to it that the British National Antarctic Expedition was organized on much the same pattern, despite marked advances having been made in the interim, particularly in clothing, cooking, and travel equipment. Most importantly, he lacked any understanding of what had proved to be the most efficient techniques for polar travel: the use of dogs to pull sledges and the utilization of skis. He passed on to Scott his prejudice against these forms of transport and his bias in favor of the grueling task of man-hauling—using teams of men in harness to pull sledges—something at which the resolute and physically powerful Scott would prove to excel. However, the weaknesses in Markham's beliefs and practices would be shown all too clearly both on Scott's first expedition and then again a decade later.

The expedition finally left Britain in the purpose-built ship *Discovery* in August 1901. They reached Cape Adare, where Borchgrevink had wintered, in January 1902, before proceeding to the Great Ice Barrier. At the far eastern end they spied a peninsula that had never been seen before, which they named King Edward VII Land. They could not reach it due to heavy ice, however, and turned back toward the west. On February 3, they landed on the Barrier and the next morning an observation balloon was filled. Claiming the right to be "the first aeronaut to make an ascent in the Antarctic regions," Scott ascended some 550 feet (168 m). He was followed aloft by the third officer of

Discovery was tucked carefully into a small bay near the hut, where she spent the next two winters (right). The party actually wintered aboard ship, while using the hut primarily for work. The hut would prove to be a major staging point for later expeditions led by Shackleton and Scott.

Expedition members were taught the basics of skiing (above), which at that time included the use of one large pole, rather than two smaller ones. As the surgeon (and primary ski instructor) Reginald Koettlitz spent more time working on the downhill technique than on that of cross-country, his efforts were not as helpful as they might otherwise have been.

Discovery, Ernest Shackleton, who rose to 650 feet (198 m) and took the first aerial photographs in the Antarctic.

The expedition now headed to McMurdo Sound, between Ross Island and Victoria Land, and at its far southern extremity they reached Cape Armitage, a peninsula where the island approached the Barrier. At a small bay nearby, Scott built his quarters, keeping the ship with them, rather than sending it north for the winter. As it turned out, the shelter that was built at what they named Hut Point was used primarily for work, while the members of the expedition lived aboard *Discovery*.

In the next several months, before the long, dark winter descended, the party fell into a routine of carrying out the necessities for living in a dangerous environment far from civilization, while at the same time conducting scientific observations. They also undertook sledge trips in order to become familiar with their surroundings. One of these—to Cape Crozier on the far side of the island—ended in disaster. When returning to base in a blinding snowstorm, a sailor named George Vince lost control on a slick surface and plunged over a cliff into the sea, never to be seen again.

Once the winter was over, the program of geographical exploration began in earnest. Unlike the German, Swedish, and Scottish expeditions, the purposes of which were primarily scientific, Scott's main focus was a journey to the south. The goal was to cross the Great Ice Barrier, a move deep into the unknown, and there was wild speculation and hope that a three-man party might be able to reach the Pole, some 730 miles (1350 km) away. After an early reconnaissance and several depot-laying efforts, the main thrust began at the start of November. In mid-November, the support party, which had been man-hauling sledges with supplies for the polar party, turned back. Three men—Scott, Shackleton, and the expedition's junior surgeon, Edward Wilson—continued on their own.

Almost immediately problems arose. The three men had brought a team of dogs, but the opening weeks of the assault on the south had shown that none of them possessed the knowledge or skills to drive them efficiently. Now, without the aid of the support party, they found that the number of dogs they had were totally inadequate for the task of hauling all the equipment and supplies that had been left behind. The men were forced to join the dogs in harness and begin the onerous task of man-hauling. Even then, the sheer amount of material was too great to move, and Scott and his companions realized the only way forward was the back-breaking task of relaying. For the next month they moved south at a snail's pace, hauling their supplies three miles (5.6 km) forward and then returning for the second half, thereby advancing only one mile (1.8 km) for each three they traveled. It was not until mid-December, when they cached part of their load, including a great deal of dog food, that they were able to advance without relaying.

The highlight of the British National Antarctic Expedition was the southern journey that began on November 2, 1902. The three members of the main southern party, Shackleton, Scott, and Wilson, are photographed in front of their sledges and their individual sledging flags.

To their disappointment, even then the journey south remained maddeningly difficult, slowed by deep snow and the dogs doing progressively less work. They were also hindered by the fact that none of the three had a sufficient understanding of the use of skis, so that, although they had brought skis with them, they were carried on the sledge rather than used. This meant that the men frequently broke through the crust of snow that, on skis, they might otherwise have glided over. The difficulties of such arduous labor were compounded by their diet; it provided neither sufficient calories for the level of energy they were expending nor the proper nutritional balance. This was emphasized when, near Christmas, Wilson observed symptoms of scurvy (a vitamin-C deficiency that can be fatal if left untreated) in his companions.

Despite their precarious condition, the three men continued south until December 30, when they camped at nearly 82° 17' S. "If this compares poorly with our hopes and expectations on leaving the ship," Scott wrote, "it is a more favourable result than we anticipated when those hopes were first blighted by the failure of the dog team."

That dog team had also paid the price. By the time the party headed north on the last day of the year, only a handful of the original 19 were still alive. These were virtually useless, and the last pair were put down two weeks later by Wilson. In the meantime, the three men slowly dragged themselves and their sledges mile after mile on the seemingly endless journey across the unending plain of ice toward the north. On January 13, 1903, with their food running out, they spotted Depot B, where they had earlier cached their supplies. Their joy was somewhat offset by Wilson's diagnosis the same day that all three men were in the advanced stages of scurvy.

Shackleton, however, was more badly affected than the other two. He was frequently short of breath, coughed persistently throughout the night, and was by far the most fatigued. Soon thereafter this reached crisis stage, and Wilson forbade him to pull the sledge. He simply had to trudge along while his two colleagues did all the pulling. This continued for much of the next two weeks, and ultimately Shackleton donned the only pair of skis they had not discarded, which greatly eased his progress.

On February 3, 1903, nearing Hut Point after their long and arduous journey deep into the heart of the Great Ice Barrier, Scott, Shackleton, and Wilson were met by two of their comrades. The engineer Reginald Skelton and the physicist Louis Bernacchi pulled the sledge back to base with ease, where the three exhausted explorers were greeted as returning heroes.

Somehow, the weary travelers continued their trudge north. On January 28, they reached Depot A, a large supply of food and oil that had been set on the Barrier the previous spring. They feasted on delicacies they had not seen in months, and their worries about starving were at an end. But they were not home yet and, as if to prove the dominance of nature, that night the heaviest blizzard of the year swept down on them. In the thick, wet air Shackleton gasped desperately for breath and became so weak that he could hardly move. The three men stayed in their tent all the next day waiting for the gale to end, but rather than the enforced break proving beneficial to him, Shackleton became progressively weaker. That night, as the blizzard continued to roar outside and he lay helpless in his sleeping bag, Shackleton heard Wilson tell Scott that he did not expect the sick man to last the night. But that comment made Shackleton determined to pull through, and the next morning, although he was incredibly weak, he was ready to travel.

The three men now plodded forward past familiar landmarks, and on February 3, they were met by colleagues from Hut Point, who pulled the sledge back to base for them. Somehow they had reached safety.

In the ensuing days, while they recovered from their ordeal, Scott, Shackleton, and Wilson found out what had occurred in their absence. Beginning in November, the expedition's second-in-command, Albert Armitage, had led a party in an attempt to scale the mountains to the west of McMurdo Sound and find a passage up to the interior plateau. The result had been the discovery of the Ferrar Glacier, which, after many trials, Armitage and a number of his men ascended. In January they had finally become the first men to reach the vast polar icecap.

Late that same month, the relief ship *Morning* had arrived. However, *Discovery* was now separated from open water by miles of ice, and after a number of attempts to free her, Scott determined to stay there a second winter. *Morning* returned north with eight members of the expedition, including Shackleton, whom Scott deemed physically unfit to remain in the south, despite the younger man's protestations.

After a second winter, Scott again led a major sledging journey, this time following in Armitage's footsteps up the Ferrar Glacier. Once at the summit, Scott struck out onto the Polar Plateau for several weeks before returning to Hut Point in order to oversee the efforts to free *Discovery* from the ice. For more than a month and a half the expedition members labored to break loose. They were joined in early January 1904 by two relief ships, *Morning* and *Terra Nova*, which came equipped with explosives and an order from the Admiralty for Scott to abandon *Discovery* if they could not free her. However, on February 16, after weeks of constant work blasting a channel some 16 miles (30 km) to the open sea, a large explosive charge loosened the last ice trapping the ship, and *Discovery* was able to escape. After two and a half years, the expedition headed home.

Shackleton's British Antarctic Expedition, 1907–09

The next attempt on the Pole was made by Ernest Shackleton, who professed little interest in science and let it be known from the outset that his goal was explorative—to reach 90° South. To do this, he planned to employ two types of transport that had never been used in the Antarctic before: Manchurian ponies and a motor-car. Before Shackleton's expedition even sailed in 1907, however, he was confronted by a claim from Scott to have the sole right to use not only the *Discovery* hut, but all of McMurdo Sound. Scott wanted to lead another Antarctic expedition, and insisted that Shackleton should not go within hundreds of miles of their old base. This was an unreasonable demand, particularly so considering that Scott had not at that time even discussed a second expedition with the Royal Navy. However, Shackleton considered Wilson a special friend, and since Wilson strongly backed Scott's position, Shackleton ultimately gave way. He promised Scott that he would make his landing at King Edward VII Land and not to go near McMurdo Sound.

But that was in London. When Shackleton's tiny ship *Nimrod* reached the Antarctic in January 1908, he found the situation not so cut and dried. The ship simply could not reach King Edward VII Land due to heavy ice, and a recent massive calving from the edge of the Barrier (a section breaking off and floating away) proved how disastrous it could be to set up a base there. So, loathe to break his promise, but feeling he had no choice, Shackleton led his men to McMurdo Sound. There the ice prevented them from reaching Hut Point, so Shackleton built a base instead at Cape Royds, 18 miles (33 km) up the coast of Ross Island.

The major problem with Cape Royds is that it is a small spit of land surrounded mostly by water and bounded on the east and southeast by the imposing slopes of Mount Erebus. These were too steep and too crevassed to allow safe passage to the south, so once the wind had blown the sea ice out of the Sound, Shackleton and his men were cut off from their goal until new ice formed. Prevented from laying depots for the Pole journey, Shackleton cast about for a task to keep his men occupied and their spirits high. The solution was obvious—they would make the first ascent of Mount Erebus (12,448 feet/3794 m). In early March 1908, five members of Shackleton's party overcame the technical difficulties of the mountain, their own inexperience and lack of equipment, and the frostbitten feet of their comrade Sir Philip Lee Brocklehurst to reach the top of the active volcano. Shackleton's party had made their first conquest.

At the close of winter, soon after the light had returned, but before the relative warmth had accompanied it, Shackleton began the process of moving supplies to Hut Point, the natural starting place for a southward journey.

In January 1904, Discovery, *still trapped in the ice, was joined by two relief ships,* Terra Nova *and* Morning. *Scott had been ordered to abandon* Discovery *if she could not be freed, but on February 16, a final explosive blast released her from the ice and allowed the expedition members to return home in their own ship.*

Shackleton brought with him an Arrol-Johnston motor-car (right), donated by William Beardmore, his initial sponsor and owner of the car-making company. Although the car played little significant role in the expedition, its presence marked a step forward in the use of modern technology in the Antarctic.

The first notable achievement of Shackleton's expedition was the ascent of Mount Erebus, which before Shackleton, had towered unconquered. In March 1908, a party of six departed from base (above) on what would become the first ascent of the snow-covered volcano.

Only three of the 15 members of the expedition had prior Antarctic sledging experience, and since it was too cold to use the ponies, circumstances forced Shackleton to introduce his men to the horrors of man-hauling. He had been obliged to readjust his plan during the winter, because he had originally calculated that he needed a minimum of six of the 15 ponies he had purchased to make the southern journey. However, only 10 ponies could fit aboard *Nimrod* and two of these had to be put down due to the battering they had taken on the voyage south. Four more had died at Cape Royds, a result of eating either the sand on which they were initially stabled or corrosive materials brought for the expedition. Shackleton had only four ponies, which meant he had to cut his southern party from six to four.

At the beginning of October, while Shackleton was laying a depot on the Barrier, three men left Cape Royds to fulfill the other major target of the expedition: reaching the South Magnetic Pole (which at that time was on land at about 71° S; constantly moving, it is now much further north, out to sea at about 65° S). This party consisted of the famed Australian geologist T. W. Edgeworth David; one of David's former students, Douglas Mawson, who would become one of the major figures in the Heroic Age of Antarctic exploration; and the Scottish surgeon Alistair Forbes Mackay. In a remarkable journey, the party man-hauled hundreds of miles up the coast of Victoria Land—relaying their loads much of the time—up onto the Polar Plateau, and thence to the Magnetic Pole, returning to the coast just in time to be picked up by *Nimrod*.

Meanwhile, the polar party—Shackleton, Jameson Adams, the surgeon Eric Marshall, and Frank Wild, who had been a seaman on *Discovery*—left Cape Royds on October 29. They soon discovered the disadvantages of using ponies rather than dogs in a glacial environment. The animals' hooves, carrying much more weight than dogs' paws, broke through the snow cover and threatened to plunge them down covered crevasses that dogs would have run lightly across. At the same time, they had to struggle constantly through snowdrifts up to their hocks and sometimes

In March 1908, a party of three was sent to climb Mount Erebus, with a support party of three more. Ultimately, the support party continued with the others, and five of the men—T. W. Edgeworth David, Douglas Mawson, Jameson Adams, Eric Marshall, and Alistair Mackay—completed the ascent, while Sir Philip Brocklehurst, who had frostbitten feet, waited for the others below the summit. Here four members of the party are seen at the crest of Mount Erebus's higher crater.

Shackleton was the first to experiment with ponies in the Antarctic. Here the four members of the southern party move ahead with their ponies each pulling a sledge. After Socks— the last of the four ponies—fell down a crevasse, the men were forced to man-haul the rest of the way.

their bellies. They also needed excessive care, having to be groomed, covered against the cold and wind, and fed large amounts of bulky fodder that had to be carried. The difficulties wore on the ponies, and one of them had to be put down a little more than three weeks after departure; this did have the advantage, however, of giving Shackleton and his companions fresh meat, which helped ward off scurvy.

By being able to pull heavier loads, the ponies did help Shackleton make much better time than when he had accompanied Scott six years before, and on November 26, the party passed Scott's farthest south, having reached that latitude in 29 days, as opposed to Scott's 59. But within a week, two more of the ponies began to fail and had to be killed, their meat either left at depots for the return journey or taken on with the men. The loss of the ponies meant that the men had to begin man-hauling, three of them pulling one sledge and Socks, the final pony, hauling another.

The Transantarctic Mountains, which had been visible to the west, now swung around in front of Shackleton's party, and in early December the men took the bold move of heading up a massive glacier that they hoped would take them through the mountains and up onto the Polar Plateau, while continuing to lead south. Soon, however, the move cost Socks his life; he plunged down a black, deep crevasse. Wild and the sledge only just escaped sharing his fate, when the harness attaching pony to sledge snapped before pulling them after him.

The four men spent the next three weeks slowly inching their way up "the Great Glacier," alternating between slick blue ice and snow-covered crevasses, at times making only a mile or two per day. By the time they exceeded an altitude of 10,000 feet (3048 m) on the Polar Plateau, they had been on partial rations for weeks, had been forced to abandon all their extra clothes because of the weight, and were becoming dehydrated from lack of oil to melt snow

Man-hauling was one of the hardest tasks ever assigned to free men (left). The heavy sledge and all its contents had to be pulled over high pressure ridges and across bottomless crevasses. Falls into the crevasses were not infrequent and the men were saved only by the harnesses attached between them and the sledges.

for water. They also faced temperatures as low as –25°F (–32°C) and strong winds blowing directly into their faces. But an indomitable spirit drove them on.

In early January, they realized that they would not be able to reach the Pole and return alive, so they made one final push to get within 100 miles (185 km). On January 9, they reached their farthest point south. "We have shot our bolt," Shackleton wrote that night, "and the tale is 88.23 S. 162 E." They had been only 97 miles (179 km) from the Pole.

Now followed one of the most dramatic stories in the history of exploration, as Shackleton's party made a desperate dash north. Time and again they ran out of food and only just staggered to the next depot—across the Plateau, down the Great Glacier, and then over the Barrier. Each man collapsed at one point or another, to be helped on by his companions. As well as being a race for survival, it was also a race against time, as Shackleton had left orders that *Nimrod* could leave for New Zealand on March 1. But somehow they made it, Shackleton and Wild stumbling into Hut Point on the night of February 28, having left an ailing Marshall a day's march back in the care of Adams. They alerted *Nimrod* of their arrival, and the next day, despite his exhaustion from months of traveling, Shackleton led the party back to rescue Adams and Marshall.

Back in civilization, Shackleton's story instantly made him an international hero. He received a knighthood, and was honored and feted throughout the British Empire and the world. In all of this, the adoring public never seemed bothered that Shackleton, Wild, Adams, and Marshall had not actually reached the Pole. But there were a select few who were much more interested in what Shackleton had not accomplished than in what he had achieved. Among these was a man who had his own plans for the attainment of the South Pole—Robert Falcon Scott.

The farthest south, at 88° 23' S on the Polar Plateau (above). Marshall took this photograph of (from the left) Adams, Wild, and Shackleton standing next to the Union Jack that Queen Alexandra had presented to Shackleton.

CHAPTER TWO

SCOTT'S FATEFUL EXPEDITION

BEAU RIFFENBURGH AND LIZ CRUWYS

SCOTT'S FATEFUL EXPEDITION

BEAU RIFFENBURGH AND LIZ CRUWYS

"A TRUE SPORTSMAN," ROBERT SCOTT SAID, raising his glass, "is not jealous of his record, or slow to praise those who surpass it." The scene was one of those that so bespeak the time that was Edwardian England. Filling the dining room of London's famed Savage Club were the glitterati of the geographical world, and sitting in the seat of honor was Ernest Shackleton.

But while Scott spoke no doubt very sincere words of praise for the achievements of his former subordinate, great must have been his inner joy at knowing that the South Pole was still surrounded by a patch of uncovered ground. In fact, while Shackleton had made speeches and presided over luncheons in New Zealand and Australia while slowly making his triumphant way back to Britain, Scott had continued with his careful planning for yet another assault on that most southerly of prizes.

So intense had Scott's early designs and strategy for another polar expedition become that, in the same week that Shackleton returned to London, Admiral Sir Lewis Beaumont, the vice-president of the Royal Geographical Society, had written a letter to the president, Major Leonard Darwin, indicating his view that the Society should stay out of any potential clash between the two explorers. The RGS, he stated, should encourage Scott to lead a scientific expedition without an emphasis on the Pole. "All of this long story is to incline you to put Scott off from making what I think will be a great mistake—that is, competing with Shackleton and organising an expedition to go over the old route merely to do that 97 miles."

Those 97 miles (179 km), however, were central to Scott's agenda, and on the evening of the very day that Admiral Beaumont wrote his letter, Scott provided a public glimpse of his intentions. In the after-dinner speech at the Savage Club, Scott turned from simply praising the commander and men of Shackleton's expedition, to urging that every future effort be made to assure that a Briton was the first to the South Pole. Indeed, he stated, he was willing "to go forth in search of that object" himself. "All I have to do now," he added, taking sardonic aim at the man he felt had betrayed him over McMurdo Sound, "is to thank Mr. Shackleton for so nobly showing the way."

Some three months later, on September 12, 1909, his intention was announced to the public, with Scott proclaiming that "the main object of the expedition is to reach the South Pole and to secure for the British Empire the honour of this achievement." For Scott himself, the aims of the expedition were not actually quite so simple. Although without formal scientific training, he had become very involved in the scientific studies carried out during his first expedition, and he was keen to ensure that a serious research program would add to the body of knowledge about the Antarctic on his next one. Yet he was not uninterested in the fame and potential fortune that could come from being the first man to reach the Pole. So, depending upon the audience to which he was speaking, he emphasized one or the other goal as the primary one, tailoring his message to attract the greatest possible public or scientific interest and funding.

The shore party (except Clissold, laid up, and Ponting, photographing) outside the hut at Cape Evans at the beginning of the fall, 1911. Standing from left: Taylor, Cherry-Garrard, Day, Nelson, Teddy Evans, Oates, Atkinson, Scott, Wright, Keohane, Gran, Lashly, Hooper, Forde, Anton, and Demetri. Sitting from left: Bowers, Meares, Debenham, Wilson, Simpson, Edgar Evans, and Crean.

During the following months, money was raised (including £20,000 from the government), the whaler *Terra Nova*—which had freed *Discovery* from the ice in 1904—was purchased and refurbished as the expedition ship, supplies and equipment were ordered, and Fridtjof Nansen was consulted. The famous Norwegian explorer who had been the first to cross the Greenland icecap and had later established a remarkable farthest north, Nansen had shown himself to be a genius at polar logistics, travel, and design of equipment. It had become one of the tasks of virtually every serious polar traveler to consult Nansen for his advice on a wide range of matters.

One of the most significant things that Nansen discussed with Scott was the proposed modes of transport toward the Pole. This was not an easy topic, because Scott had decided that several distinct methods would be used together. Nansen's recommendation was that the British expedition should follow the pattern of the most successful efforts in the Arctic and use skis in conjunction with dogs pulling sledges. Although Scott acquiesced regarding skis in the face of Nansen's arguments—and as the result of a demonstration of their efficiency when used by an expert—he was less than wholehearted about the use of dogs, undoubtedly recalling the problems he had encountered with them on his first expedition. He would take dogs, but it was only late in the expedition that he realized how well they could perform when expertly handled, and that he had brought too few to accomplish all the heavy pulling tasks they might have done.

Part of Scott's hope was placed on tracked motor sledges, which Commander Reginald Skelton, the former engineer of *Discovery*, had been helping to design, develop, and test for the previous two years. Despite the difficulties encountered on his first expedition, Scott also expected to man-haul. But the proposed method of transport that Nansen simply could not understand was the one that followed Shackleton's example of using Manchurian ponies. He argued strongly against them being taken. Nevertheless, ignoring the numerous difficulties with ponies that had been revealed all too clearly by his predecessor, Scott rather quixotically adopted them as a major part of his grand plan, going so far as to order only white ponies, because Shackleton's lighter ponies had lived longer than the darker ones.

Meanwhile, the naval officers and crew and scientific staff were also being selected. This was no easy task, as the expedition office received more than 8,000 applications. One of the first men invited to go had been Wilson, who was eventually named chief of the scientific staff, zoologist, and expedition artist. Part of his duty was to help Scott put together a large, well-equipped scientific team that would be able to carry out research at a variety of locations.

Oates with some of the 19 Manchurian ponies that were taken to the Antarctic for Scott's expedition.

A great help to them in this was T. W. Edgeworth David, the renowned professor of geology at the University of Sydney, who had led the party that had been first to reach the South Magnetic Pole on Shackleton's *Nimrod* expedition. One of the men Scott desperately wanted to join the expedition was David's former student Douglas Mawson, who had made major contributions to Shackleton's expedition. Although he decided to organize his own expedition instead, Scott's entire geological complement was eventually composed of David's former students or men who had worked under him: Griffith Taylor, Frank Debenham, and Raymond Priestley.

The scientific staff also included two biologists: Edward Nelson, who would be part of the land party, and Dennis Lillie, who would remain aboard *Terra Nova* when she sailed back to New Zealand and then returned the following year to pick up those who wintered in the Antarctic. The meteorologist was Dr. George Simpson, on loan from the Indian Weather Bureau, and the physicist was the Canadian Charles Wright. As assistant zoologist, Scott was finally persuaded to accept Apsley Cherry-Garrard, the cousin of Reginald Smith, Scott's publisher and friend. Cherry, as he became known, had no scientific qualifications but was a protégé of Wilson, and this, together with the fact that he offered to pay £1,000 to join the expedition, persuaded Scott to take him.

Funding had also played an important role in the selection of two other members of the expedition. The first of these was the 28-year-old Royal Navy Lieutenant E. R. G. R. "Teddy" Evans, who had been second officer aboard *Morning* on the relief expeditions for *Discovery*. He had begun to organize an expedition of his own before being united with Scott by Markham, who recognized in the energetic Evans the ability to interest potential contributors and to raise more much-needed money. In return for being named second-in-command, Evans abandoned his own plans, added the funds he had already raised to those for Scott's expedition, and took over the supervision of the refurbishing, customizing, and stocking of *Terra Nova*. Unfortunately, their totally different temperaments meant that the two men would never be close, and there would exist between them only an uneasy alliance.

The other man whose involvement in the expedition was in part due to his money was a captain in the 6th Inniskilling Dragoons: Lawrence Edward Grace Oates, who soon came to be known as "Titus" by the other expedition members. An upper-class cavalry officer who had received a serious wound in the leg during the South African War, Oates offered £1,000 and his services for free should he be accepted. His love of and expertise with horses made him a natural to serve as the man in charge of the ponies.

Strangely, however, Oates's expertise was not used to its full advantage. He proved to be such a hard-working addition aboard *Terra Nova* during her preparations that Evans asked Scott if he could be kept aboard as a midshipman rather than being sent to Siberia to select the ponies. Scott agreed, but it was a critical error. Those who went instead were Cecil Meares—a superb dog-driver who had joined the expedition as the man in charge of the dogs—and, to help bring the animals from Vladivostok to New Zealand, Wilfred Bruce, Scott's brother-in-law. Despite his expertise with dogs, Meares knew little about horses. Thus, the ponies selected were, according to Oates when he saw them later, an exceptionally sad lot—too old, too diseased, too lame, and too full of a catalogue of other defects to be adequate for the work they would be expected to carry out.

Just as problems arose with the ponies before the expedition sailed for the Antarctic from New Zealand, the motor sledges also suffered an early setback. Once in place, Evans told Scott that he did not feel it appropriate that Skelton, who outranked him, should be serving under a junior officer. In response to Evans's concern, in March 1910, Scott released Skelton, who felt slighted after more or less being promised the position of second-in-command himself. Ultimately more significant was that Skelton was the only man on the expedition who really understood the motor sledges. His successor, Bernard Day—who had been in charge of Shackleton's motor-car on his 1907–09 expedition—never was as familiar, efficient, or productive with the motor sledges as Skelton.

Some six weeks before the expedition was due to sail, three other key officers joined the ship. Lieutenant Victor Campbell, who was to be the acting first mate, was a martinet with a short fuse and an explosive temper, but one who proved a remarkably efficient officer. Lieutenant Henry Bowers of the Royal Indian Marines, the officer in charge of supplies, had a seemingly infinite capacity for hard work and was a master of meticulous planning. And Lieutenant Harry Pennell was named navigator and was placed in charge of the ship's magnetic work. Considered by Wilson to be "by far the most capable man on the whole expedition," Pennell would ultimately take command of *Terra Nova* once the shore party had been left in the Antarctic.

The *Terra Nova* Sets Sail

On June 15, 1910, *Terra Nova* sailed from Cardiff, where she had put in for her last stop in Britain. This was a sign of appreciation both for the large contributions raised there for the expedition's coffers and for generous donations of coal, oil, and scientific equipment. The master of the ship was Evans, as Scott had decided to remain in England to continue raising funds. Two months later, when the barque that Wilson described as having two speeds—"slow and slower"—arrived at Simonstown, South Africa, they were met by Scott, who had arrived by (fast) steamer. The first two months under Evans had been a relatively lighthearted time in which the men had taken the opportunity to get to know each other. Now, with "the Owner" (as Scott was jocularly referred to) assuming command, the expedition took on a much more serious tone, as he began to assess those aboard in order to determine who would join the land party and who would remain with the ship.

One early determination was that Campbell would lead the so-called Eastern Party. Scott's plan was for there to be, in essence, two shore parties. The major one, to winter in McMurdo Sound as close to Hut Point as possible, would include both the members of the Polar Party and the majority of the scientists, several of whom would go to nearby sites of special scientific interest, such as Dry Valley (now known as Taylor Valley). A smaller party, consisting of Campbell and five other men, was to be landed on King Edward VII Land, which had been seen by earlier expeditions but never actually reached. This meant that the members of the Eastern Party would be in an even

As Terra Nova *entered the pack, the men aboard had no idea how long they were to be unexpectedly slowed down. Here, three members of the expedition survey the pancake ice stretching off into the distance.*

better position to make new geographical discoveries than those with Scott. Who would belong to which party, or remain with the ship, was therefore a topic of great interest for everyone. But as the ship sailed slowly toward Australia, Scott, as later he would do throughout the expedition, kept his own counsel on personnel assignments, and announced them only in his own time.

On October 12, *Terra Nova* arrived at Melbourne, and suddenly Scott had other, alarming things to ponder. Waiting for him was a message that he read with puzzlement and then increasing irritation. "Beg leave to inform you," it stated, "*Fram* proceeding Antarctic. Amundsen."

What did it mean? No one was certain. It was common knowledge that Roald Amundsen, the Norwegian explorer who several years before had become the first man to navigate the Northwest Passage, had borrowed Nansen's ship *Fram* to make a polar drift in the Arctic basin. His goal had been to be the first man to the North Pole, and, although that possibility seemed to disappear when the Americans Frederick A. Cook and Robert E. Peary had independently claimed to have attained the Pole in September 1909, Amundsen had steadfastly stuck to his plan. Or so it had seemed. Now Scott questioned Tryggve Gran—the young Norwegian he had hired as a ski expert at Nansen's recommendation—but he knew no more than anyone else.

It would be more than two weeks—by which time Evans had taken *Terra Nova* to the harbor of Lyttelton, New Zealand, and Scott had reached that dominion's capital of Wellington after trying to raise funds on a trip across Australia—before they began to hear rumors of a challenge for the Pole. But they were just that: rumors. There was little hard evidence. Was Amundsen trying to beat Scott to the base in McMurdo Sound? Was he heading to the Weddell Sea on the far side of the continent? No one knew for sure. But at that point Amundsen's behavior, although an annoyance and a subject for a debate on the ethics of exploration, was not seen as a threat by most of the members of the British expedition. There was one man, however, who took a very different view, realizing that Amundsen was quite capable of snatching the Pole from the grasp of the British. "If he gets to the Pole first we shall come home with our tails between our legs and no mistake," Oates wrote in a letter to his mother. "They say Amundsen has been underhand in the way he has gone about it but I personally don't see it is underhand to keep your mouth shut—I myself think these Norskies are a very tough lot … they are very good ski-runners while we can only walk, if Scott does anything silly such as underfeeding his ponies he will be beaten as sure as death."

Three days after Oates wrote those words, *Terra Nova* sailed for Port Chalmers, at the bottom of New Zealand's South Island, to take on a final supply of coal before heading for the Antarctic. There was hardly any room left aboard for it. During the weeks in Lyttelton, more had been forced into the holds and tied down on the decks than would have been believed possible when they left Britain. After Bowers had recounted and restowed the supplies already aboard, he oversaw the packing of tons of food and other materials donated by the generous New Zealanders. Then the three motor sledges in their huge crates were lifted aboard.

Shortly before departure, the 19 Manchurian ponies that had been held in quarantine on Quail Island in Lyttelton Harbour since their arrival from Russia were placed in stables that had been constructed on the ship's upper deck and under the fo'c'sle. Oates felt the amount of fodder that had been purchased for the animals was woefully inadequate, and managed to persuade Scott to increase it, before also cleverly loading an additional five tons he had paid for himself. Meanwhile, Meares constructed places on deck for his 33 Siberian sledge dogs, and then had to find quarters for himself, Bruce, and two Russians who had helped them transport all the animals from Vladivostok: the jockey Anton Omelchenko, who was to serve as a groom for the ponies, and Demetri Gerof, an experienced dog-driver who would help handle the dogs.

Also joining in New Zealand (and therefore packing the ship even tighter) were the Australia-based contingent—Taylor, Debenham, Priestley, and Day—as well as an itinerant photographer whom Scott had employed to make a careful record of the expedition. His name was Herbert Ponting but, although he was celebrated for the wonderful photographs he had taken throughout the world and had just that year published the fine photographic book *In Lotus-Land: Japan*, he preferred to be known, not simply as a photographer, but as the grander sounding "camera artist."

There were undoubtedly members of the expedition who initially had their doubts about Ponting, as he seemed fussy, prim, and demanding. As he later wrote in his book *The Great White South*: "Life on the *Terra Nova* was a very different matter to travelling on comfortable ocean liners"—the kind of observation that would have done little to endear him to men who had spent years at sea in difficult conditions. And to a crew working shifts and sleeping in hammocks located directly beneath the leaky planking where the ponies were stabled, it would have seemed strange that this fastidious man "found it almost impossible to sleep below deck in the narrow, stuffy cabins, crowded with our personal belongings." It would not be long, however, before the photographer Herbert Ponting won the respect of his shipmates, engaging

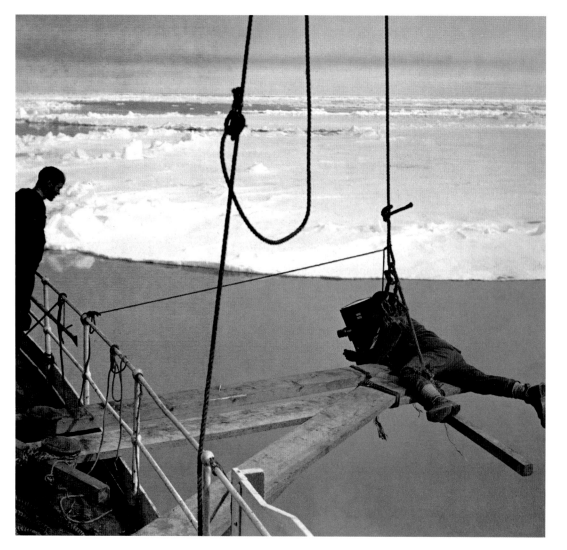

When *Terra Nova* reached the pack ice on her way south, Ponting willingly took risks to make his record of the journey. Three planks were extended 10 feet (3 m) from the ship to form a small platform on which he could lie with his cinematograph, in order to film the ship's battles with the ice. He had to grasp the camera with one hand, and turn its handle with the other, hoping not to be thrown into the slush below.

in all manner of contortionist efforts to obtain the best possible photographs and footage with his cinematographic camera. He climbed the rigging in high winds; had a specially designed frame placed over the side of the ship so that he could film with his moving-picture camera from what proved to be a most precarious position; and he worked all times of day and night to record the members, events, and general images of the expedition. He quickly changed from an oddity to a highly valued colleague.

Terra Nova was just two days out of Port Chalmers when a gale of enormous proportions swept down on the heavily laden ship and almost ended the expedition before it even reached the Antarctic. Giant bags of coal and canisters of oil hurtled about the deck as huge waves broke clear over the top of the ship. The main pump failed, and all available men had to be set to bailing, a chain of hands passing buckets of water out of the boiler room, which was quickly filling with water, and up to the deck.

The ship was, in fact, slowly filling with water and sinking, and no amount of human bailing was going to keep it from disappearing into the depths of the ocean. The pump simply had to be repaired. But it proved impossible to open the hatch to the pump, so 12 agonizing hours were spent creating another path to its suction well. A hole was cut through the engine-room bulkhead, some of the coal in this next compartment was removed, and another hole was cut from there into the suction well. Teddy Evans then wriggled past the remaining coal, squeezed through the small hole, and found his way down the pump shaft. He cleared the suction mechanism of the coal balls that had formed from a mixture of coal and oil, and, free from this choking mixture, "to the joy of all a good stream of water came from the pump for the first time." The ship had been saved, although not without some cost. Two ponies, one dog, 10 tons of coal, and 65 gallons of petrol had been lost.

As the ship headed south, Scott began giving serious consideration to landing the main part of the expedition at Cape Crozier, at the eastern end of Ross Island, rather than in McMurdo Sound at its western end. This would allow them to land earlier, since they would not have to wait for the ice to clear out of the Sound; it would mean that the sea ice (or lack of it) would not affect the summer depot parties, as it had Shackleton's; it would give direct access to the Barrier at a point with fewer crevasses than the route south from McMurdo; and it would allow Wilson the opportunity to study the unknown behavior and incubation of the nearby Emperor penguins.

Before such considerations could be taken into account, however, *Terra Nova* faced another problem. On December 7, the first ice was sighted, and although this excited the men, it was considerably farther north than had been expected. Two days later the ship entered the pack ice that protected the northern reaches of the Ross Sea.

Terra Nova's passage through the pack ice took much longer than Scott had anticipated. One of the few benefits of the time she was held captive in the ice was the chance it gave Ponting to take a wealth of marvelous photographs. This one clearly shows the difficulties an old wooden ship would have trying to force its way through heavy pack ice.

Scott had expected to move through the pack rapidly, as it had taken only four days for *Discovery* to pass it and even less for *Nimrod*. But fortune did not smile on Scott this time. For 20 days *Terra Nova* remained mired in the midst of the ice, at times moving so slowly that Gran was able to begin training his comrades in the use of skis on nearby floes. It was only early in the morning of December 30 that the ship was finally free of the ice and plying its way south through the rough Antarctic waters. More than time had been lost—it had taken 61 tons of coal to break through the pack, and that would have an impact on how long the ship could remain in the south and how far she could transport various landing parties later.

Several days later another disappointment awaited. The heavy swell at Cape Crozier made disembarkation impossible, and Scott reluctantly ordered a turn to the west and McMurdo Sound. Perhaps the most disappointed of the party was Ponting, who had been promised the chance to photograph and film the Barrier. But the extra time spent in the ice meant that coal was too precious for such non-compulsory ventures. "With a heavy heart I then impotently watched the bastioned rampart slowly disappear astern," Ponting later wrote, adding, "one of the most remarkable features of the Earth, to see which, and in the hope of illustrating it … I had come over more than a third of the circumference of the globe."

The Base at Cape Evans

They now made good time to McMurdo Sound, and on January 4, 1911, finding the way to Cape Armitage blocked by ice, Scott decided to establish his base at a small promontory that had been dubbed "the Skuary" during his previous expedition (since it was a nesting ground for large numbers of skuas), a dozen miles or so north of Hut Point. This he immediately renamed Cape Evans in honor of his second-in-command.

The work of unloading began immediately, the ponies and dogs being taken to shore that day, as well as two of the motor sledges and most of the prefabricated elements for the hut that would house them through the winter. For the next week the members of the expedition were very busy. While the hut was being built, the pulling power of ponies, dogs, and sledges was used to take the stores ashore.

The ponies and dogs were off-loaded before the supplies, because there were fears for their health after being cooped up for so long in small spaces without proper exercise. The ponies caused particular concern, and two had been so badly battered on the voyage south that they had to be destroyed. The dogs were passed over the side in a sling-like contraption, while the ponies were lowered in crates.

On January 8, however, disaster struck. On this day it was decided to unload the third of the motor sledges and take it ashore. In the days that had passed since the other sledges had been unloaded, the ice had thawed and become progressively weaker, and the third sledge plunged through one such weak point—over which, only the day before, one of the other sledges had hauled a heavy load. None of the men hauling the motor sledge was injured but, according to Scott, "It's a big blow to know that one of the two best motors, on which so much time and trouble have been spent, now lies at the bottom of the sea."

The same week a second calamity on the sea ice was narrowly averted. Ponting, who was constantly recording the events of the moment, went onto an ice floe to photograph a pod of killer whales. Undoubtedly thinking him a seal, the killer whales bumped the bottom of the floe in order to knock him into the water—typical behavior for the giant predators. The floe broke and Ponting leapt to the next one, pursued by the voracious killers. As his comrades looked on helplessly, the camera artist managed to scramble with his camera from floe to floe just out of reach of the killer whale's hungry jaws. "What irony of fate to be eaten by a whale thinking one was a seal," Campbell wrote to his sister after Ponting's escape, "and then be spat out because one was only a photographer." Ponting would not have been pleased.

By January 18 the hut—a spacious 50 feet (15.2 m) long by 25 feet (7.6 m) wide—was ready to be occupied. It was divided into two major sections, with officers and "lower deck" segregated by a wall of packing cases. But the layout of the accommodation mattered little at that stage, because only a limited number of men would initially remain there. With no time to waste before the summer began to wane and the cold, dark winter drew on, Scott had no fewer than four parties setting out from Cape Evans.

Scott left first, with a group of 12 men, eight ponies, and two dog teams, making their way south to Hut Point and thence onto the Barrier to lay depots in preparation for the next spring's attempt on the Pole. The next departure shortly thereafter was the five-man Western Party led by Griffith Taylor and consisting of Debenham, Wright, Petty Officers Edgar Evans, and Robert Forde. This headed for the mountains on the western side of McMurdo Sound to make a geological examination of the region between Dry Valley and the Koettlitz Glacier. Meanwhile, a four-man party consisting of Ponting, Day, the biologist Nelson, and Chief Stoker Bill Lashly, was to go on a 10-day photographic trip to Cape Royds.

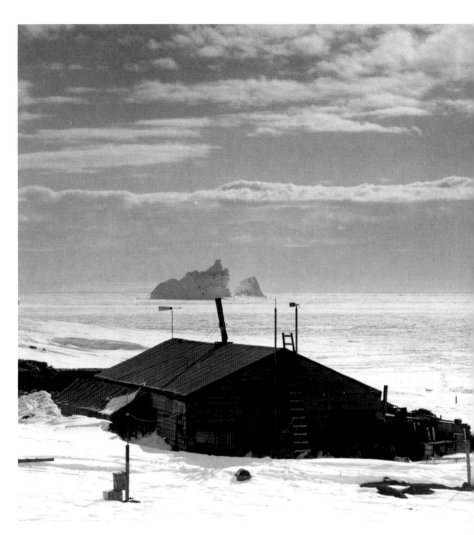

It might not look like much, but the hut at Cape Evans seemed like paradise to the members of the expedition whenever they ventured away from it, particularly on long sledging journeys. Today, the hut still stands strong and proud in its desolate location, but it is accompanied by an eerie feeling of tragedy, as if it still remembers what happened so long ago.

The final group was the six-man Eastern Party under Campbell, which consisted of the geologist Priestley, the surgeon Murray Levick, Petty Officers George Abbott and Frank Browning, and Able Seaman Harry Dickason. After dropping off Taylor and his colleagues, *Terra Nova* made for King Edward VII Land, where Campbell's small party was to be landed. The intention was that, following the erection of a hut, they would set out to discover as much as possible both geographically and scientifically about the region. But after proceeding along the Great Ice Barrier, they found that there would be no possibility at all of reaching their destination, which was surrounded by vast fields of sea ice interspersed with countless icebergs. They reluctantly turned back west, hoping to find some point where they could land on the Great Ice Barrier.

On February 3, *Terra Nova* sailed into the indentation in the Barrier that three years before Shackleton had named the Bay of Whales. Campbell had hoped it would make a good landing place, but to his horror he found it already occupied. There, nestling against the ice edge, was *Fram*. Amundsen had not only come to the Ross Sea, but was firmly ensconced in a camp three miles (5.6 km) inland, having arrived at the Barrier three weeks previously. The following day Amundsen visited *Terra Nova* and invited Campbell, Pennell, and Levick to breakfast at his base, which he had named Framheim. The British explorers were impressed by the magnificence of the Norwegians' temporary home, which included a sauna, a massive library, and a carefully designed setup for some 110 dogs. They were also well aware that Framheim's location placed Amundsen a full 60 miles (111 km)—one whole degree— closer to the Pole than was Scott based at Cape Evans.

In this photograph, Ponting has captured the natural beauty of Antarctica as well as the laborious daily tasks undertaken by the men.

Roald Amundsen's carefully designed base, Framheim, at the edge of the Great Ice Barrier. The members of the Eastern Party found Amundsen's expedition ensconced here in February 1911, a discovery that helped lead to the decision for the Eastern Party to become the Northern Party.

Amundsen generously offered to share his facilities with the members of the British expedition, should they wish to winter at the Bay of Whales, but Campbell would not consider such a course, and they continued west along the Barrier hoping to find another suitable site. They could not, however, and on February 5, they made for McMurdo to report the situation to Scott and the main body of the expedition. Scott had not returned, so after taking steps to ensure he would be informed at the earliest possible moment, Campbell and his party sailed north. Both Campbell and Pennell were anxious not only to find a location in which the newly redesignated Northern Party could winter, but also for the ship to leave before it became too late in the season to escape the ice.

In mid-February, Campbell and the five men in his charge were left at Cape Adare, where, close to Borchgrevink's old hut, they built one of their own. Perhaps it was just as well for their own peace of mind as they worked that they could have no inkling of the fact that before they were to be reunited with the rest of the expedition they were to experience two difficult winters, enduring in one of them some of the most difficult survival conditions in the history of Antarctic exploration.

Scott, meanwhile, had taken his party south with the intention of setting up several depots at intervals along the Barrier. These were to be stocked with sledging rations, oil for cooking, and food for the ponies and dogs. His goal was to place these depots as far out from their base as 80° S. In the early stages of the journey, the dogs performed magnificently, but the ponies showed not only the problems of their breed in such an environment, but also the ill effects of being battered by the weather and sea while aboard ship. The men had brought one set of a type of snowshoe adapted for the ponies, and these worked like a dream on the animal named Weary Willie. However, when Meares and Wilson attempted to go back to Cape Evans for more of them, they found that the sea ice had broken up, leaving them unable to reach their base.

The party headed south and east, establishing depots at what they named Safety Camp, and then Corner Camp. This was on the same longitude as Cape Crozier, and the intention was to aim directly south from there toward the Beardmore Glacier, which Shackleton's party had ascended to the Polar Plateau, thereby missing a dangerous series of crevasses on the direct route across the Barrier from McMurdo to the glacier. After being held up for three days by a blizzard, the party made its way south to 79°, where they established Bluff Depot.

Significant problems soon developed, however, as the ponies began to show serious signs of deterioration, despite having been out for less than three weeks. Oates argued that in their current condition the ponies would be unable to return to Hut Point, so the most productive plan would be to take them as far south as possible, and then to kill them and depot the meat for use the next spring by the men and dogs of the Polar Party. Scott felt this was inhumane, and refused. He sent three of the weaker ponies back with Teddy Evans and two of the men.

Shortly thereafter, distressed by the suffering of the remaining five ponies, Scott decided to leave the rest of the supplies at what they named One Ton Depot, located at 79° 29' S, some 30 miles (56 km) short of the point they had originally hoped to reach. Oates, who took a more pragmatic view of the ponies than Scott, again argued that all effort should be made to move the supplies as far south as possible, regardless of the cost to the animals. Again, Scott refused.

After they stowed the supplies, Scott, Wilson, Cherry-Garrard, and Meares began their return with the dogs, leaving Oates, Bowers, and Gran to bring back the five exhausted ponies. When the dog party reached Safety Camp, however, they found that only one of Evans's three ponies had survived the return journey. Worse yet, Atkinson, the surgeon who had been left behind on the outward journey with a foot injury, had returned to Hut Point, where he had found a letter from Campbell telling of the discovery of Amundsen. He passed the letter to an angry and worried Scott, who was made even more frustrated by being on the Barrier with no way back to base until the sea froze over again. For the first time, it became obvious to Scott that time was not on his side and that he was now in a race for the Pole.

While Scott was still weighing his options regarding the Norwegian threat, Oates and company arrived at Safety Camp with all five ponies, but that very night Weary Willie died. This emphasized the fact that Scott would have to allow for better conditions for the remaining ponies the next spring, meaning that he would require a later start than originally planned, which in turn, he feared, would give Amundsen an even greater head start than the 60-mile (111-km) advantage he already had. He decided, however, that "the proper, as well as the wiser, course for us is to proceed exactly as though this had not happened."

In the meantime, however, the party needed to reach the safety of Hut Point, and Meares and Wilson returned with the dog teams while Bowers, Cherry-Garrard, and Petty Officer Tom Crean continued with the remaining four ponies. After a day of exhausting and difficult travel, near the edge of the Barrier, the three camped on what proved to be unstable ice. They awoke, according to Bowers, to find: "We were in the middle of a floating pack of

On April 13, 1911, having spent about a month at Hut Point waiting for the ice of McMurdo Sound to refreeze and allow them to return to Cape Evans, Scott and his men—a motley party if ever there was one— returned to their base. Those returning included both members of the depot-laying party and Taylor's first Western Party, which had engaged in a geological survey in the Western Mountains.

broken-up ice." One of the ponies had already disappeared, and while Crean raced back to Scott and Oates for help, Bowers and Cherry-Garrard desperately tried to get the other three ponies back to the Barrier. But although the men eventually reached safety, and were able to bring one pony with them, the other two ponies fell in the water, where Oates and Bowers ultimately had to kill them with pickaxes to prevent them from being devoured alive by killer whales.

Not only had Scott's party lost six of their ponies, but the men now found themselves cut off from Cape Evans. They could do nothing but move into the old *Discovery* Hut, where on March 15, they were joined by Taylor's party returning from the Western Mountains. The hut was inadequately supplied and organized for so many men, contributing to the frustrations of an already tense period. Everyone was anxious to return to Cape Evans—which now seemed a virtual oasis in their memories—and almost immediately upon the formation of the new sea ice, Scott and Evans led parties those final few miles back north. They arrived at their base on April 13, only 10 days before the sun rose for the last time, presaging a winter that for some of them would be colder, darker, and more terrible than anything they had ever experienced.

Winter at Cape Evans

Although the disappearance of the Sun mostly confined the members of the British expedition to Cape Evans, the area within and around the hut became a hive of activity. A vast array of scientific observations was made, most notably by the brilliant meteorologist Dr. George "Sunny Jim" Simpson. Part of the hut was designated as the scientists' workshop—over-generously called "laboratories"—where studies of zoology, parasitology, physics, and geology were conducted. Next to this area was the 6 by 8 foot (1.8 by 2.4 m) darkroom where Ponting not only carried out much of his work, but also slept, in company with the constant smell of photographic chemicals.

In addition to the all-important scientific program, there was a large amount of work to be done both to prepare for the spring's sledging journeys and simply to exist, day to day, in such a hostile environment. But all activities were not solely devoted to the completion of tasks; the members of the expedition found time to enjoy themselves as well. Special dinners were held whenever a suitable occasion allowed, and birthdays in particular were celebrated with great gusto. Midwinter Day, on June 22, was the highlight of the season, and was treated in the same manner as Christmas.

A Sunday service was held each week, and a variety of musical instruments had been brought south, including a pianola on which Debenham and Cherry-Garrard particularly excelled, and a banjo that Ponting played regularly (despite Griffith Taylor's comment that only Ponting was a worse musician than himself). Cherry-Garrard served as editor of the *South Polar Times*, an expedition magazine that was continued from its original appearance on Scott's first expedition. Scott also introduced a series of evening lectures, which proved not only valuable but exceptionally popular: Scott presented his plans for the following spring and summer; Wilson talked about painting, drawing, and birds; Oates taught the men how to take care of the ponies; and the scientists each discussed their specific areas of expertise.

Perhaps the favorite of these evening talks, however, were those given by Ponting, who accompanied them with showings of his exquisite lantern slides that had been taken all over the world. "Ponting would have been a great asset to our party if only on account of his lectures," Scott wrote in his diary, "but his value as a pictorial recorder of events becomes daily more apparent. No expedition has ever been illustrated so extensively."

Indeed, although his duties seemed on the surface physically light in comparison to those of many members of the expedition—who complained that he was simply doing photographic work while they were hauling materials ashore and building the hut—few worked harder or longer than Ponting. No aspect of the expedition or the environment escaped his cameras, still or moving, whether it was the natural beauty of the Antarctic, the laborious daily tasks of the men, the life of the dogs, ponies, and wildlife, or the preparations for the great sledging journeys. And photographing, developing, or printing in

One corner of the hut at Cape Evans (left) was allotted to the scientific staff to aid them in their work. One of the busiest members of the expedition was the biologist Nelson, shown here in his "biological laboratory."

the dark, freezing conditions of the Antarctic were no simple tasks. Few comments are more illustrative of the difficulties that could be encountered than an example given in *The Great White South*: "On another occasion, my tongue came into contact with the metal part of one of my cameras, whilst moistening my lips as I was focusing. It froze fast instantaneously; and to release myself I had to jerk it away, leaving the skin of the end of my tongue sticking to my camera, and my mouth bled so profusely that I had to gag it with a handkerchief."

The man who was nicknamed "Ponco" by the other expedition members expected the subjects of his photographs to give just as great an effort as he did. He could be very annoying in demanding the men hold poses for an extended period of time, particularly during periods of little light and great cold. "The photographer Ponting is an abominable nuisance," the physicist Wright wrote, "we have to be posing the whole time for his cinematograph… There are two of the men, Levick and Meares, [who] are always being photographed. I have not yet discovered whether they like it or are merely more obliging than the rest of us." Ponting's insistence on such cooperation led Griffith Taylor to invent a new verb for him: "to pont," meaning "to pose, until nearly frozen, in all sorts of uncomfortable positions."

Nevertheless, throughout the year in which Ponting was in the Antarctic, he had Scott's full blessing and cooperation. Scott was hoping to use both Ponting's photographs and his moving film to publicize the expedition and to help contribute to its coffers. In fact, Ponting would only find out when he returned to England that the rights to his photographs had been sold without his knowledge.

Music and entertainment were important parts of expedition life (above). Meares poses at the pianola, although only Cherry-Garrard and Debenham had any genuine skill on the instrument. Ponting played the banjo (badly) and sang.

In the middle of the winter of 1911, three men made the trip to Cape Crozier that was later immortalized as "the worst journey in the world." From left: Birdie Bowers, Edward Wilson, and Apsley Cherry-Garrard shortly before their departure to study the incubation of Emperor penguins and to collect some of their eggs. The journey turned into a nightmare, and the three men were lucky to return alive.

Two of Ponting's most famous photographs were of the members of a party that made a sledging trip during that winter, an excursion that has since become immortalized as "the worst journey in the world." Ever since Scott's first expedition, Wilson had wanted to make a winter visit to the Emperor penguin colony at Cape Crozier, in order to study the incubation of the birds and to collect their eggs. It was his hope that studying the Emperor penguin embryos would establish that a link existed between birds and dinosaurs, and he wanted to test theories connecting their feathers to reptilian scales. The inability to land and establish base near Cape Crozier meant that the only way to obtain the eggs necessary for the study was to make a sledge journey there in the middle of winter, soon after they had been laid.

Thus, on the morning of June 27, Wilson, Bowers, and Cherry-Garrard set off on the 58-mile (107-km) trip to the Emperor penguin colony on Cape Crozier. They knew from the outset that their journey would be brutally difficult, involving as it did hauling food and equipment on two sledges that totaled 757 pounds (343 kg) in weight, traveling over rough ice, in the dark, and experiencing some of the coldest temperatures on Earth.

Crossing Ross Island directly was impossible because of the presence of Mount Erebus, so the party went south past Cape Armitage, onto the Great Ice Barrier, and then turned northeast. Once on the Barrier, the temperatures became even colder, soon dropping to -56°F (-49°C). But that was just the beginning. At such low temperatures they could not budge the sledges on the rough surface of the Barrier, so they had to relay, hauling first one sledge and then returning for the other, dropping their progress to little better than a crawl. But even worse than the brutally hard work during the day was the time they spent in their sleeping bags at night. They froze, they shivered, their bodies cramping from the ice that continuously formed on the bags, both during the day when they were on the sledge and at night as they lay inside them.

Horrifically, the temperatures plummeted even further, reaching a low of -77°F (-61°C) on July 5, and at times not rising above -60°F (-51°C) at even the warmest time of the day. But somehow the three men struggled on, reaching their goal on July 15. Here, on a slope above the penguin colony, they built a small camp consisting of their tent and a stone igloo, the roof of which was a piece of canvas.

On July 20, they made a tortuous descent to the penguin colony, killed three penguins so that they could use the blubber to supplement their limited heating oil, and collected five eggs, two of which were broken on the climb back to the igloo. But their plans to collect more eggs were terminated when a gale made the conditions outside impossible. As they huddled in their igloo, an exceptionally strong gust blew their tent away. Knowing they could not survive the return journey without it, the three hurried out into the blizzard, but it was gone. Yet, as desperate as their situation was, it soon became worse, when their canvas roof was also destroyed by the wind. The three men retired to their icy sleeping bags to pray, sing hymns, and hope for salvation.

When the gale died down, they had no choice but to search for the tent, and remarkably, Bowers found it about a quarter of a mile away. They quickly set out for home. The journey was no easier than on the way out, but the three men persevered, and on July 31 they reached Hut Point. The next night, after pushing themselves beyond what they believed they could do, they arrived at Cape Evans, where they had to be pulled forcefully out of their clothes, which had long since frozen in place on their bodies. Their journey had taken them 116 miles (215 km) in 36 days, but they had been perhaps the harshest, most demanding days in the history of Antarctic exploration. Ponting took the famous picture of the three men around the table immediately following their return—such a contrast with the sturdy, confident image he had taken at their departure on June 27—and he later wrote: "their faces bore unmistakable evidence of the terrible hardships they had endured. Their looks haunted me for days."

The Push to the Pole

On November 1, Scott and nine of his comrades, leading 10 ponies, departed from Cape Evans on the first stage of their journey toward the South Pole. Guiding them were the tracks of the two motor sledges, which had left base on October 24, hauling three sledges each and loaded with food, fuel, and equipment. Scott's orders to Teddy Evans, in command of the motor sledges, had been to proceed to Corner Camp, on to One Ton Depot, and thence due south to 80° 30' S, where they would rendezvous with Scott's pony party. Meares and Demetri were to follow Scott

A map of Scott's route on his journey to the South Pole, showing where he and his colleagues camped each night. It also marks the location where each supporting party turned back, and where the members of the Polar Party died.

later, with 23 dogs hauling two sledges. Initially, Demetri took Ponting to the edge of the Barrier, so that he could use his cinematograph to take film of the men on their journey south with the ponies.

The procession, which ultimately numbered 16 men, 10 ponies, and 23 dogs, did not last long in its planned form, however. On November 4, before they even reached Corner Camp, the pony leaders passed one of the motor sledges, which was irretrievably broken down and abandoned. Two days later, Scott's party found the remains of the abandoned second motor sledge. Evans and his three companions—Day, Lashly, and the steward F. J. Hooper—had moved ahead taking the most valuable of the supplies from the motor sledges by man-hauling. The experiment with modern technology had proven a failure, as Oates grumpily noted after a gloomy conversation with Meares: "We both damned the motors. 3 motors at £1,000 each, 19 ponies at £5 each, 32 dogs at 30/– each. If Scott fails to get to the Pole, he jolly well deserves it."

Captain Scott and some of the members of the Polar Party and the support party pose in front of Mount Erebus during the early stages of the Southern Journey.

The unhappiness of Oates was brought about not only by the failure of the motors, but by the poor condition of the ponies—something he had regularly commented on since he had first seen them in New Zealand. He also observed the comparative ease with which Meares and Demetri brought the vibrant dog team into camp each day. It quickly became obvious that the dogs, which many of the expedition members had dismissed as a virtual irrelevancy, were the most efficient form of transport in the Antarctic environment. But with less than a quarter of the number of dogs that Amundsen had at his disposal, it was too late to do anything about it. Meanwhile, Scott made the decision that no attempt would be made to take the ponies up the Beardmore Glacier. Only enough fodder would be taken to get them to its foot, where any remaining would be killed.

On November 21, the three elements of the Southern Party were united, when pony and dog teams arrived at the point where Teddy Evans had been instructed to meet them. This became known as the Mount Hooper Depot (after Frederick Hooper, one of Evans's team) in ironic honor of the monstrous cairn that Evans and his comrades had built there while waiting for the others to arrive.

The daily progress now spread across the Barrier, as five separate starts were made after each night's camp. Evans's man-hauling team left two to three hours before those leading the ponies, who departed in three teams, based on the condition of their four-legged companions. Finally, several hours after the last of the ponies had gone, Meares, Demetri, and the dogs set out. Three days after the start of this pattern, the first pony was shot, and its leader, the surgeon Atkinson, joined the man-hauling team. At the same point, Day and Hooper were sent back to Cape Evans with a sledge and two sick dogs.

On November 26, the Mid-Barrier Depot was established at 81° 35' S. Two days after this the man-hauling team received a very welcome helping hand when Wright, the physicist, joined them after his pony was put down. The next afternoon, they passed Scott's original farthest south, which he had set almost nine years before. Not only was this an emotional and psychological boost for them all, but also they began receiving the physiological benefits from eating the pony meat—which added essential vitamins that the pre-prepared pemmican, biscuit, and other elements of their normal diet did not provide.

By early December, five of the 10 ponies had been shot, but despite heavy snow, which had slowed the progress of the remaining ponies dreadfully, the party had crept near to The Gateway—the entrance to the Beardmore Glacier. Scott hoped that the next day would see them on the glacier itself. But it was not to be, as a warm gale blew with such ferocity that they were kept in their camp for four days. All were miserable, as the temperature rose to the point where pools of water formed around and under the tents and everyone became soaked.

When the blizzard ceased, the party moved painfully forward to The Gateway. But the terrible storm had taken virtually all of the strength out of the ponies, which had to be flogged to keep moving. That night, at what was named "Shambles Camp," the remaining ponies were killed. The act brought a strange sense of relief to many of the party, their thoughts being recorded by Wilson, when he wrote: "Thank God the horses are now all done with and we begin the heavier work ourselves."

When Amundsen and his fellow Norwegians—Olav Bjaaland, Helmer Hanssen, Sverre Hassel, and Oscar Wisting—arrived in the region of the South Pole, they made many careful observations to assure themselves that they had reached the Pole. Here they take readings at the Pole, the Norwegian flag beside them.

That work began on December 10, although the three new man-hauling units were not totally on their own until Meares and Demetri had helped set up the Lower Glacier Depot the following day. Meares then turned north and sped away with the still rambunctious dogs. The three man-hauling teams, of four men each, comprised Scott, Wilson, Oates, and Petty Officer Edgar Evans; Teddy Evans, Atkinson, Wright, and Lashly; and Bowers, Cherry-Garrard, and Petty Officers Crean and Keohane. Almost immediately the second group began to show more signs of exhaustion than the other two, but this was natural as all four men had been pulling for a considerable length of time already, while the others had only been leading the ponies.

The men now engaged in harder work than most of them had imagined possible, slogging their way ahead with 700 to 800 pounds (318 to 363 kg) per sledge, up a ceaseless grade that would prove to be about 105 miles (195 km) long and would rise eventually to more than 10,000 feet (3,048 m) above sea level. On December 13, they pulled until 7:00 in the evening but managed only 4 miles (7.4 km) for the day.

Three days later, conditions had not improved much, and Scott was beginning to show concern in his diary. "We must push on all we can, for we are now 6 days behind Shackleton," he wrote, mentioning, as he did frequently, the ghostly rival against whose timetable in 1908–09 he seemed always to compare his efforts.

It was ironic that Scott seemed more concerned with Shackleton than with Amundsen. The latter was now far to the south. On December 7, while Scott and his companions were trapped in their tents during the storm, Amundsen and his team, skiing across the Polar Plateau, had also thought of Shackleton. That day, they had surpassed his farthest south—an achievement which they rejoiced while giving honor to their predecessors. "We did not pass that spot," wrote Amundsen, "without according our highest tribute of admiration to the man, who—together with his gallant companions—had planted his country's flag so infinitely nearer to the goal than any of his precursors. Sir Ernest Shackleton's name will always be written in the annals of Antarctic exploration in letters of fire."

And so, indeed, would Amundsen's. For at the very moment Scott wrote about being behind Shackleton's pace, Amundsen and his four fellow Norwegians—Olav Bjaaland, Helmer Hanssen, Sverre Hassel, and Oscar Wisting—

44

were at the South Pole. Two days before that, they had become the first men ever to reach it, and on December 17, they left the tent they had named Polheim in order to begin their return to civilization, having taken the prize that Scott so desperately wanted.

In the meantime, the members of the British expedition continued their slow, grinding ascent of the Beardmore. On December 21, after a particularly long and difficult march, they reached the location where they established their Upper Glacier Depot, at 85° 7' S. The next morning the four men Scott considered the weakest were sent back: Atkinson, Cherry-Garrard, Wright, and Keohane. Actually, few of the men were in particularly good shape, and Oates was feeling as poorly as any of them. He was having problems both with his old thigh wound and with his feet, about which he wrote: "They have been continually wet since leaving Hut Point and now walking along this hard ice in frozen crampons has made rather hay of them." Atkinson, who was closest to Oates on the expedition, was later to tell Cherry-Garrard that Oates had not wanted to continue, but had been unwilling to disclose this to Scott. This was typical of the time, when physical weakness was seen as something to be ashamed of and when suffering in silence was considered the duty of a brave man. Oates was undoubtedly the most stoic member of the expedition, and he was not about to reveal his inner thoughts to Scott in such a situation.

Scott gave Atkinson one important instruction before they parted company. Scott and Meares had quarreled before the latter had turned back, and Meares had indicated that he was going to return home on *Terra Nova*, which was likely to sail before Scott's party returned to Cape Evans. Scott now instructed Atkinson to bring the dogs south later in the season in order to meet the Polar Party on its way back. It appears that Scott had developed concerns about recrossing the vast Barrier to One Ton Depot. After having dismissed them for so long, he now saw the dogs as providing the margin of error for his return.

Meanwhile, as they crossed the upper parts of the glacier, Scott's group stayed intact, while Evans and Lashly made up a new team with Crean and Bowers. Leaving behind the Upper Glacier Depot did not mean that the eight remaining men had reached a level plain and were going to have an easy time. Their route continued uphill, on and on, for more than two weeks. Even Christmas Day did not bring a break, although they did have special meals to celebrate. Scott, who was arguably the physically most powerful of the group, seemed driven as if by demons that day, and led a particularly long and difficult march, which left even the usually imperturbable Bowers exhausted. "My breath kept fogging my glasses, and our windproofs got oppressively warm and altogether things were pretty rotten," Bowers wrote. "At last [Scott] stopped and we found we had done 14 miles. He said, 'What about fifteen miles for Christmas Day?' so we gladly went on—anything definite is better than indefinite trudging."

It was not necessarily the best strategy. Although the men did their best to keep up with their chief, they were gradually wearing out, and Bowers noted that they were all getting thinner. They were suffering from a combination of factors: lack of caloric intake, dehydration, low temperatures, and high altitude. Members of both sledging teams were having difficulties.

Oscar Wisting and his dog team at the South Pole. After spending two days in the vicinity of the Pole, Amundsen and his men headed back north toward Framheim—and immortality.

Scott at the time seems to have focused on the problems affecting Teddy Evans's team, and on December 31, he ordered them to depot their skis and continue on foot. In retrospect, this was a strange decision, because Scott had acknowledged that it was easier to travel on skis, and two days later he wrote, "It's been a plod for the foot people and pretty easy going for us." Why he made this decision has never been fully answered. The same night, he made his final decision about who would accompany him to the Pole.

On the morning of January 3, Scott told Teddy Evans, Crean, and Lashly that they would not be part of the final Polar Party, following which he announced a remarkable change of plans by asking Evans to return with just the two men, allowing Bowers to join the Polar Party. Under the circumstances of command, Evans could hardly refuse.

Scott's decision to proceed with five men instead of four has never been fully understood, and it has been the subject of controversy for decades. It threw out the logistical planning that had been carefully followed so far, it meant that Evans's party would be seriously undermanned on the return, and it left Scott with an extra mouth to feed and another body to cram into their already small tent. So why did Scott make such a decision? Although he may have calculated that a fifth man's strength in pulling the sledge would outweigh the difficulties such a change might bring, it appears that it was an emotional, rather impulsive decision.

There had been little doubt that Wilson, Scott's companion on his previous farthest south and his confidant, as well as one of the strongest of the party, would be selected for the final push to the Pole. Bowers, although not initially one of Scott's coterie, had proven himself invaluable as a navigator, the man in charge of stores, a tireless worker, and unquestioningly a devoted follower of "the Owner." So Wilson and Bowers being named members of the final party was no surprise. However, the selections of Oates and Edgar Evans were, in retrospect, less than logical. The choice of Oates appears to have been greatly dictated by the fact that Scott, as the leader of a naval expedition, wanted a representative of the other great service—the army—to join him at the Pole. Oates had also proven his value by his indefatigable work with the ponies, but in the later stages of the journey he had increasingly suffered from problems with his feet and from his old war wound, which had left his left leg several inches shorter than the right and had made the long journey particularly difficult. In addition, his extra work with the ponies during the journey to the Beardmore had meant that he had worked longer hours than his comrades and had missed numerous meals. He was worn down, his strength and stamina sapped, and his desire to attain the Pole was not as all-encompassing as that of several of his comrades. Oates would give the final journey everything he had, but the problem was that too much of his energy had already been expended.

One of the reasons for selecting Edgar Evans had been similar to that for Oates: Scott wanted the lower deck, as well as officers, represented at the Pole. But although Evans was a large, powerful man whose very physique gave confidence in his abilities and who had utter devotion to his leader—a feeling that was reciprocated—his drinking in recent years had undoubtedly taken a toll, and Wilson had expressed doubts about his ability to perform under stress. In fact, Wilson and Atkinson had agreed, shortly before Atkinson turned back, that Lashly—a teetotaler and non-smoker—was by far the best choice of the seamen, and it appears that Crean was in better shape than Evans as well. But Scott's personal regard for Evans seems to have influenced his decision.

Thus, on January 4, a party of five continued south. One of the problems with the change of plan had already arisen, as Bowers—having been one of the group ordered to depot their skis—was forced to plod along on his short legs while his companions had the advantage of using skis. Moreover, they soon found it took considerably longer to cook for five than for four, meaning that they would run out of fuel much more quickly. Because he was forced to keep up with the men on skis, Bowers soon found himself perpetually exhausted. And Evans began to have

The final Polar Party man-hauling on the Plateau. Taken by Bowers (who had no skis), this picture shows (from left): Evans, Oates, Wilson, and Scott only days before they discovered that Amundsen's party had beaten them to the South Pole.

problems with his hand, which he had cut seriously on December 31 when he and Crean had been attempting to change the sledge runners from 12 feet to 10 feet (3.7 m to 3 m) in order to lighten the load.

These problems did not seem of overarching significance, however—and certainly not when compared to the fact that they were drawing steadily nearer to the Pole. Besides, Scott undoubtedly felt added security in the verbal instructions he had sent back with Teddy Evans for yet another change in the plan for the dogs. In the middle of February, Scott now ordered, Meares was to bring the dogs to between 82° and 83° S to meet the Polar Party— much farther south than previously planned—and assist them in returning in time to catch *Terra Nova*. That there would be plenty of time for the instructions to be followed, Scott had no doubt, as he noted when he saw Evans, Crean, and Lashly head north: "I was glad to find their sledge is a mere nothing to them, and thus, no doubt, they will make a quick journey back." Unfortunately, he was wrong, and it would have dire consequences for his party.

A Tragic End

As Scott and his four companions continued south, Teddy Evans, Crean, and Lashly were having no easy time of it, struggling along the hundreds of miles to Cape Evans. The journey back down the Beardmore Glacier was a nightmare, as even the hard-as-nails Lashly admitted. "I cannot describe the maze we got into and the hairbreadth escapes we have had," he wrote. "The more we tried to get clear the worse the pressure got; at times it seemed almost impossible for us to get along."

The situation was made still worse when Evans went snow-blind after removing his goggles to try to find a safe path to follow. It meant that he was unable to pull the sledge, and had to walk nearby, condemning the two others to unbelievable daily hardships. When they finally did reach the bottom of the glacier on January 22, it became apparent that Evans was suffering from the advanced stages of scurvy. He became progressively weaker, and by the beginning of February had to be strapped onto his skis. Then, in the middle of the month, he suddenly passed out in the middle of a march, to the great alarm of Crean and Lashly, who initially thought he had died.

The two exhausted, overburdened seamen now made a choice that only those with compassion as great as their strength could make. They discarded everything they felt they could live without, and strapped Evans onto the sledge. Ignoring his pleas to be left behind, they hauled him mile after mile, day after day, across the Barrier. Their hopes soared when they reached the southernmost of the motor sledges and they knew they were not far from Corner Camp. But the next morning, Evans could not even be moved. With nothing else they could do, Lashly stayed with his commander, and Crean walked on alone to find help. More than 30 miles (56 km) later, at 3:30 on the morning of February 19, he staggered into Hut Point. Fortunately, Atkinson and Demetri were there with the dog teams in order to restock One Ton Depot. If the old hut had been empty, Evans would surely have died.

As it was, Atkinson had to wait until the next afternoon before setting out on his rescue mission, because a sudden fog made traveling with the dogs too unsafe. As soon as the conditions cleared, they raced out to pick up the sick man and his intrepid nurse. With constant attention from Atkinson in the ensuing weeks, Evans survived. However, his condition could well have contributed to an apparent failure of Scott's message about the dogs going to meet the Polar Party being passed along. It is uncertain where in the chain of command the message was lost or forgotten, but Evans was soon taken out of the equation, because when *Terra Nova* arrived, he was loaded aboard and taken back to New Zealand to recover. His saviors, Crean and Lashly, were each later awarded the Albert Medal for their remarkable and heroic actions.

The successful efforts of the two men to save Evans caused a feeling of elation among the expedition members still at Cape Evans. This was buoyed even more when Crean and Lashly reported that the five members of the Polar Party had seemed healthy and strong when they left them. It was perhaps only Gran who had the premonition that things were not working out as well as planned. To him, Evans's condition told a story much more frightening than the others seemed to realize.

"My conversation with Evans had not lasted long, but from what I heard," he later wrote, "the prospects of our five-man polar party were not so bright as most of the members of the expedition imagined. Evans's frightful return journey was a pointer to what Scott and his men would be bound to undergo." Sadly, all the joyful optimism was misplaced, and it was Gran's pessimism that would prove to be correct.

Far to the south, Scott's party had made steady progress, and on January 9 they passed Shackleton's record, three years to the day after it had been established. But Shackleton had possessed the wisdom to know that this was as far as his party could safely go, and had the courage to turn back despite being so close to the Pole. Even then, he and his companions had only just made it home alive. On the same day of the year, Scott's party—cold, exhausted, undernourished, dehydrated, and undoubtedly already suffering from scurvy—continued south.

After another week of struggle, on the night of January 16 Scott wrote: "The worst has happened." He went on to record how they had seen a black feature ahead, which, as they approached, turned out to be "a black flag tied to a sledge bearer; near by the remains of a camp; sledge tracks and ski tracks going and coming and the clear trace of dogs' paws—many dogs. This told us the whole story. The Norwegians have forestalled us and are first at the Pole."

It was a heartbreaking discovery, made no easier to bear the next day when they reached the vicinity of the Pole itself. "Great God! this is an awful place," wrote Scott, "and terrible enough for us to have laboured to it without the reward of priority." They continued to make observations on January 18, in the process finding the tent the

The posture of the members of the Polar Party says it all, photographed after their arrival at Polheim, the Norwegian tent near the South Pole. Amundsen left a note for Scott asking him to forward a letter to the King of Norway should the Norwegian party not return safely. Later found with the journals and letters of Scott, Wilson, and Bowers, the letter proved beyond doubt that Amundsen's party had won the race to the South Pole.

Norwegians had left behind. Within it was a record of the party that had been there, an assortment of items the Norwegians did not want to take back with them, and a note to Scott asking him to forward an enclosed letter to the King of Norway, should Amundsen's party not return safely themselves. The disappointed British explorers took pictures of themselves at the Pole and dejectedly headed north. "Now for the run home and a desperate struggle," Scott wrote. "I wonder if we can do it."

It appeared for a while that they would. They kept up a steady march, sometimes helped by the wind from the south, in front of which they rigged sails on their sledges. On the last day of January they found Bowers's skis, which meant he could now move across the snow as easily as his comrades. But at the same time, the constant cold, depression, and the effects of scurvy and malnutrition were beginning to take their toll on all of them. Moreover, a series of injuries started to plague them. Oates's toes turned black from frostbite, Wilson strained a tendon in his leg, and Evans's fingernails began to come off. His hands were already raw and sore, and the hand where he had cut himself would not heal. Even worse for them all, the big petty officer began to suffer a noticeable decline in both his physical ability and his spirit.

On February 7, the party reached the Upper Glacier Depot and were able to breathe a collective sigh of relief that they were now off the dreadful Plateau. Conditions, they believed, would soon improve. Parts of each of the next two days were spent "geologising"—collecting rocks for later study—and although they made little progress northward, there must have been some satisfaction for them in continuing the scientific program that had been such a major goal of the expedition from its inception.

A moment of triumph was turned into one of bitter and heartbreaking disappointment when Scott's party found that Amundsen and his companions had destroyed their hopes of being the first men to reach the South Pole. Before turning dejectedly north, they took a series of pictures of themselves at their own tent at what they figured to be the Pole. In the photograph (right), the five doughty explorers in a row are (from left) Wilson, Scott, Evans, Oates, and Bowers. In the photograph (opposite), the agony of destroyed hope is reflected in their faces. Sitting are Evans and Oates, while behind them stand Bowers, Scott, and Wilson.

However, things got back to normal—that is, terrible—on February 11. The five men went from an area of massive pressure ridges to one comprised of a maze of crevasses. The next day was more of the same as, according to Wilson, they wandered about "absolutely lost for hours and hours." By that evening, they were down to one meal left in the food bag. They received a temporary reprieve the next day when Wilson spied the flag of the Mid-Glacier Depot, but even that only gave them three and a half days' food.

In the following days, as they struggled down the tortuous glacier, Evans went into a serious decline. "Evans has nearly broken down in brain, we think," Scott wrote on February 16. "He is absolutely changed from his normal self-reliant self." Scott had hoped that Evans's condition would improve as they went down the Beardmore and approached the Barrier, but instead he simply collapsed. On February 17, his comrades allowed him to follow them out of harness, but even without having to pull a load he soon dropped far behind. When they returned to find him, he was on his knees with his hands uncovered and was totally disoriented. They put him on a sledge and brought him to camp, but he quickly became comatose, and that night he died. "It is a terrible thing to lose a companion in this way," Scott wrote in his diary, "but calm reflection shows that there could not have been a better ending to the terrible anxieties of the past week."

Indeed, although they mourned the loss of their comrade, Evans would only have continued to slow the progress they were struggling so hard to make. As it was, the next day the reduced party managed to reach Shambles Camp, having left the glacier behind. They dined on large amounts of horsemeat, and their hopes rose. But they were still separated from their destination by hundreds of miles, and they soon found the surface of the Barrier so difficult as sometimes to limit their movement to only 5 miles (9.3 km) a day. Then, the temperatures dropped fiercely, reaching -40°F (-40°C) on the night of February 27.

To Sir George Egerton

My dear Sir George

I fear we have shot our bolt — but we have been to the Pole + done the longest journey on record

I hope these letters may find their destination some day

Satisfactory reasons of our failure to return are due to the sickness of different members of the party — but the real thing that has stopped us is the awful weather and unexpected cold towards the end of the journey

This resource of the Barrier has been fully three times as severe as any experience we had on the summit

There is no accounting for it but the result has thrown out my calculation + here we are little more than 100 miles from the base + petering out

Goodbye — Please see my widow is looked after as far as Admiralty is concerned

R Scott

My kindest regards to Lady Egerton
I can never forget all your kindness

On March 1, the men dragged themselves into the Mid-Barrier Depot, only to discover that there was a serious shortage of oil (much of it having evaporated), and that they would be lucky to have enough to reach the next depot. Moreover, that day, after more than two months of troubles, Oates revealed the appalling state of his badly frostbitten and now gangrenous feet. They were not his only problem. The body needs vitamin C to keep scar tissue together, and the scar on Oates's thigh, a legacy from his service in the South African War, appeared to have begun to dissolve, and the wound to reopen. The three other members of the party were also suffering from scurvy, but Oates's pain must have been truly horrific.

Yet still they crawled across the seemingly endless Barrier, all of them growing progressively weaker with Oates soon no longer being able to help pull the sledge. On March 9, they reached the Mount Hooper Depot, but to their great dismay, it had not been restocked as Scott had hoped. "Shortage on our allowance all round," he wrote. "The dogs which would have been our salvation have evidently failed." In fact, because Scott's final message had never been passed on, and he had earlier forbidden Atkinson to risk the dogs by a longer journey (wishing to preserve them for further sledging the following season), the animals had not been taken past One Ton Depot, where for six days they had been waiting with Cherry-Garrard and Demetri. In terrible conditions of low temperature and wind, the party advanced slowly, but it finally became too much for Oates. On March 15, he asked to be left behind in his sleeping bag, but his comrades would not do it, so he managed another few miles.

But the next morning, when he woke, according to Scott, "It was blowing a blizzard. He said, 'I am just going outside and may be some time.' He went out into the blizzard, and we have not seen him since… We knew that poor Oates was walking to his death, but though we tried to dissuade him, we knew it was the act of a brave man and an English gentleman. We all hope to meet the end with a similar spirit, and assuredly the end is not far."

It was not. Despite Scott's own feet now having become severely frostbitten, the three men staggered on to a point only 11 miles (20 km) south of One Ton Depot. But there a severe blizzard blew in, halting their progress. They agreed to move after it abated, but it continued and as the three weak men ran out of their remaining food and strength, all they could do was await the end in their tent.

Before he died—it is thought to have been on March 29, although that is uncertain—Scott's last major act was to write a series of letters and a message to the public, justifying his decisions and the manner in which the expedition had been run. Despite all of the difficulties they had faced, and their approaching end, he was still able to state straightforwardly that: "for my own sake I do not regret this journey, which has shown that Englishmen can endure hardships, help one another, and meet death with as great a fortitude as ever in the past."

Then, as the endless blizzard outside threatened to hide them and their achievements forever from the world, with remarkable prescience Scott wrote: "Had we lived, I should have had a tale to tell of the hardihood, endurance, and courage of my companions which would have stirred the heart of every Englishman. These rough notes and our dead bodies must tell the tale…."

The memorial cross erected at Observation Hill, overlooking Hut Point and the Great Ice Barrier. Made of jarrah, an Australian hard wood, the cross is 9 feet (2.7 m) high.

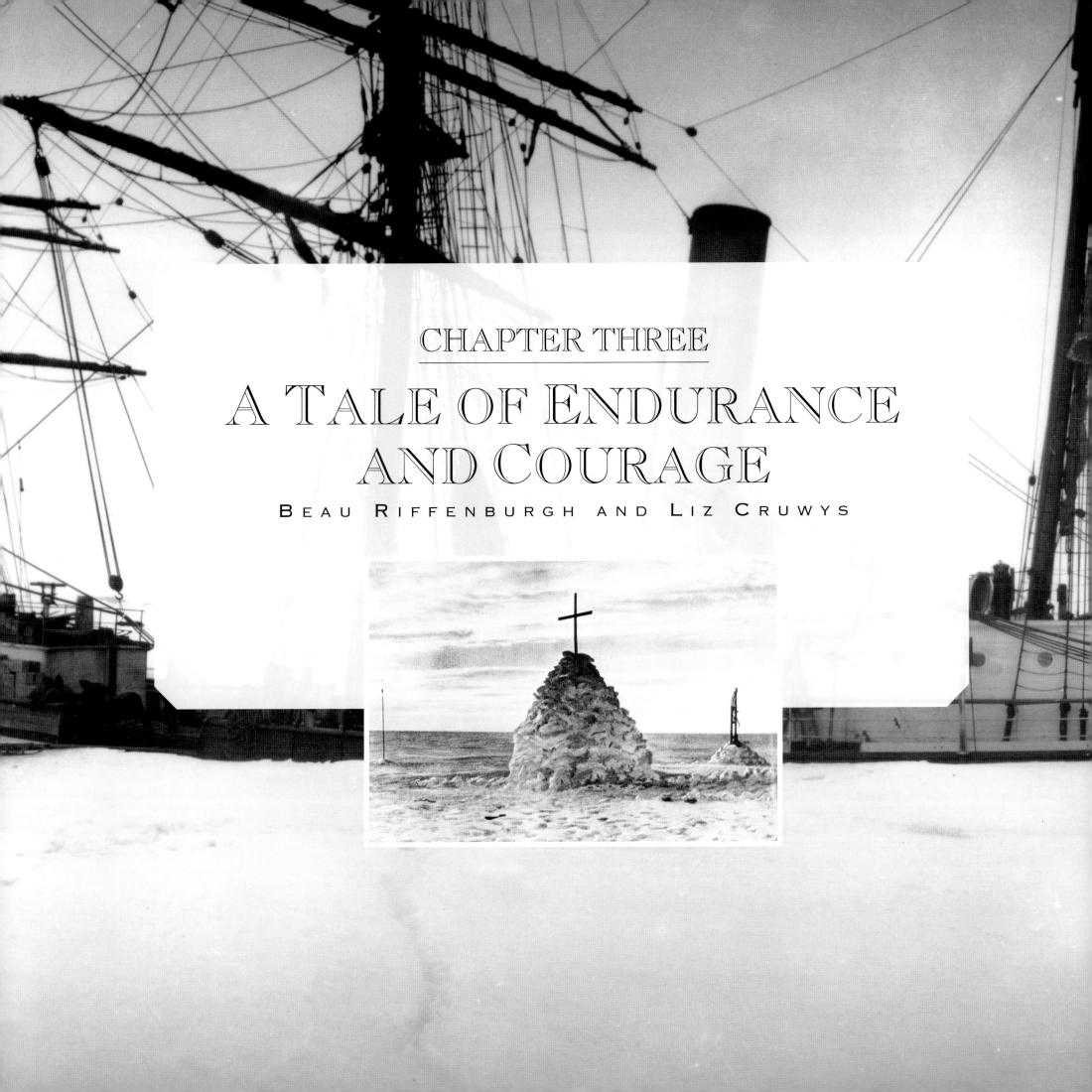

CHAPTER THREE

A Tale of Endurance and Courage

Beau Riffenburgh and Liz Cruwys

A TALE OF ENDURANCE AND COURAGE

BEAU RIFFENBURGH AND LIZ CRUWYS

On Midwinter Day—June 22, 1912—Dr. Atkinson, who, because of his seniority was, rather unexpectedly, the leader of the small group left wintering at Cape Evans, gave his men the opportunity to discuss what should be the priorities of the coming spring. After much deliberation, their eventual decision was unanimous. As soon as the conditions allowed, they would travel south in an effort to discover what had been the fate of their friends in the Polar Party.

It had not been an easy choice to make because, as Apsley Cherry-Garrard had indicated at the beginning of the winter, "it seemed to me unthinkable that we should leave live men to search for those who were dead." Indeed, that any such decision would even have been necessary was not something any of them had anticipated, and had been brought about by a remarkably unfortunate chain of events.

For two days, the men of the Northern Party and Terra Nova's crew worked almost unceasingly to unload the components of the hut and the tons of stores that the party would need for a long winter at Cape Adare. Campbell and his men realized that this was not an ideal place, but time was against a change of plan or the pursuit of a better location, so they remained, knowing they would not be picked up for one year.

The Northern Party's small hut at Cape Adare was erected next to Borchgrevink's old base. Built in haste with some assistance from Francis Davies, Terra Nova's *leading shipwright, the hut proved effective during the Northern Party's stay, but has not weathered since as well as Scott's primary huts.*

A major part of the tale had begun when *Terra Nova* had sailed north in February 1911 with the six members of what had become the Northern Party. In the middle of that month they were dropped off at Cape Adare in Victoria Land, where Carsten Borchgrevink had previously wintered, their main objective being to engage in a detailed investigation of the areas around Cape North. This was a previously unexamined region of the Antarctic coast to the west of Cape Adare. The geographical and scientific work that was planned for the vicinity would be similar to that which had been intended for King Edward VII Land.

With the help of crew members from *Terra Nova*, Borchgrevink's two prefabricated huts were restored, and a small new hut was built for the wintering party. Then the ship sailed away, leaving behind Victor Campbell and his carefully chosen party. This consisted of the naval surgeon Murray Levick; the geologist Raymond Priestley, who was afforded honorary officer status; and three seamen: Petty Officer George Abbott, Petty Officer Frank Browning, and Able Seaman Harry Dickason.

The members of the Northern Party quickly settled into a routine that included geological, microbiological, zoological, and magnetic observations, as well as round-the-clock meteorological measurements. They also had to fulfill the duties necessary for a day-to-day existence, with Abbott proving to be a talented carpenter and Dickason an excellent cook and baker. But by the beginning of May, the winter was upon them, announced by a ferocious and prolonged blizzard. Throughout the winter Campbell—who had been nicknamed the "wicked mate" for his nasty temper—maintained order and structure for the party with firm discipline and an unyielding routine.

This map of the coast of South Victoria Land (right) includes the Northern Party's route south on its return to Cape Evans from Inexpressible Island. The inset (above) shows detail of the region of Cape Adare and of the sledge trips on Robertson Bay.

But he chafed at the enforced idleness of the long darkness, and on July 29—well before the spring had truly appeared—he led Priestley and Abbott out on the first sledging journey.

The original plan had been for the six men to divide into two parties for a venture that would cross Robertson Bay—the 25-mile- (46-km-) long basin that separated Cape Adare from Cape Barrow to the west—and explore the unknown regions beyond that, toward Cape North. But early training journeys showed this to be impossible because the heavy salt content in the bay ice made sledging so slow that adequate supplies could not be taken.

Then, in the middle of August, a gale blew much of the ice out of the bay, meaning that the traveling party would have to pick its way carefully along the coast, much of which was covered by huge glaciers backed by large mountains. Following this route, Campbell's party was eventually stopped well short of its goal by mushy, thin ice. They were alerted to the danger of this only when they heard a seal gnawing the ice below them as it made itself an air hole—proving that the surface over which they were walking was far from safe.

Amidst the broken remains of icebergs, pancake ice formed on Robertson Bay and the other areas near Cape Adare. The lonely figure on the ice indicates how difficult it was to attempt to travel over such variable conditions.

Because of this breakup of the ice, the men were essentially trapped at Cape Adare for most of the late spring and summer, although they continued their scientific observations. Levick was able to make sufficient notes and take enough pictures to enable him upon his return to Britain to produce a book entitled *Antarctic Penguins*. The stay at Cape Adare ended abruptly when *Terra Nova* appeared on January 3, 1912. Pennell, commanding the ship, was concerned because at Robertson Bay, as he later wrote, "the tidal streams are strong, the pack ice heavy, there are very many grounded bergs about, and gales are frequent and fierce, while the uneven bottom suggests the likelihood of unknown pinnacled rocks." So he made all haste to bring the six men aboard. After several hours, heavy pack ice pushing toward the shore forced him to put back out to sea and the boarding operation was not completed until the next day. Even then, safety issues did not allow them to load all of their carefully assembled scientific samples, much to the dismay of the shore party. Levick in particular was disappointed, as the penguin skins he had prepared and his taxidermist's equipment were left behind.

The lack of ability to travel meant that Campbell and his party had not achieved the goals with which they had set out. Desperate to show something for his command, Campbell had Pennell drop his party off near Evans Coves in Terra Nova Bay, along the Victoria Land coast. The plan was for them to be collected six weeks later, after the members of the Second Western Party—Griffith Taylor's geological survey in the area of Granite Harbour, across McMurdo Sound from Ross Island—had also been picked up. But with Campbell anxious to get on with his exploration, and Pennell concerned about the safety of his ship, a decision was made that almost proved disastrous. "We had prepared a large depot at Cape Adare which was to have been landed with us here," Priestley later wrote, "but it was necessary to sledge all our gear about half a mile over sea ice before it would have been possible to depot it [at the new location], and as Campbell did not wish to delay the ship, he decided to land only such spare food as could be taken in one journey by ourselves and a sledge party from the ship's crew."

The spare food to which Priestley referred consisted only of those supplies that were deemed necessary in the event of *Terra Nova* returning later than its planned date of February 18. Campbell considered this possibility highly unlikely. Thus, in addition to the six weeks' sledging rations, the party had only a month's skeleton rations and a small amount of other emergency fare. They did not now concern themselves with what seemed unimportant issues, and quickly set out to explore and survey their surroundings. In the following weeks, they made long sledge journeys and compiled several scientific collections, the most important of which included segments of fossilized tree trunks, found in sandstone deposits, indicating the warmer climatic conditions of Antarctica's past.

M̄an-hauling across Robertson Bay was no easy task for members of the Northern Party. The bay ice was heavily impregnated with salt from the sea, which made sledging so slow and difficult that the men could not haul enough supplies to allow them to make a journey of any significant distance.

In early February, the six men returned to their depot to await the ship. *Terra Nova* did not come. As the days went by, they gradually became less casual about its failure to arrive, and began to worry that something disastrous had befallen it. In fact, it was not until February 15 that Pennell had been able to pick up Griffith Taylor and the other members of the Second Western Party. He then turned *Terra Nova* north and made an effort to reach Campbell's small group. But well south and east of Terra Nova Bay they met heavy pack ice and, after several efforts to penetrate it proved futile, the ship returned to Cape Evans. At this stage, communication between any members of the expedition was extremely difficult, because the wind had blown the ice out of the end of McMurdo Sound, cutting off Cape Evans from Hut Point.

When *Terra Nova* appeared off Hut Point, Atkinson took Teddy Evans, still gravely ill, aboard, where he continued to take care of his patient. Because Atkinson had to remain with Evans, he was not able to go south with the dog team to meet the Polar Party, as Scott had instructed him, and on February 28, he instead sent Cherry-Garrard and Demetri. The two men reached One Ton Depot on March 4; almost immediately a blizzard hit and temperatures dropped sharply. For four days they were trapped in atrocious conditions, until, when the blizzard finally blew itself out, a lack of dog biscuits meant that the dogs would have to return north after only another two days. The foul weather had taken its toll on the dogs, so Cherry-Garrard chose to remain in camp rather than travel farther south. He did this in response to Scott's instructions from the early stage of the Southern Journey (Scott's later revised instructions not having reached him), which were not to risk the dogs in any way. Therefore, on March 10, Cherry-Garrard turned north, arriving at Hut Point six days later.

In the meantime, *Terra Nova* had made another attempt to reach Campbell's party. Again, the effort had failed. Owing to a dwindling coal supply, the ship could not remain in McMurdo Sound later than March 8, so Pennell dropped off Atkinson and Petty Officer Keohane at Hut Point and made a final attempt to rescue the Northern Party. After failing yet again, *Terra Nova* headed toward New Zealand, with not only Evans aboard, but also a number of the shore party who had planned to remain only for one year and now had to return north for other duties, including Ponting, Meares, Day, Taylor, and the meteorologist Simpson.

Late in March, Atkinson again tried to assist the Polar Party. Unable to take Demetri or Cherry-Garrard—who were not yet well enough to sledge—and still cut off from Cape Evans, he went south with Keohane. They passed

Corner Camp on March 29, the day that Scott made the final entry in his journal. But the conditions let them go no farther, and they returned to Hut Point. Soon after that, they crossed fragile new sea ice to Cape Evans.

Atkinson now organized an attempt to rescue Campbell, an act that showed great determination, not only because of the difficulties of the time of year, but also because he was uncertain whether they needed rescuing; for all he knew they might have been collected by *Terra Nova* at the third attempt on her way north. As winter neared, Atkinson, the physicist Wright, Keohane, and Petty Officer Williamson (who had joined the shore party for its second winter when other men returned home) marched across the frozen Sound and attempted to go north along the coastline. They could find no trace of their comrades, and returned to Hut Point on April 23, the last day they saw the Sun for four months. As winter descended on those members of the expedition remaining in McMurdo Sound—without knowing for certain which of their friends were still alive—the hut seemed almost deserted.

How the Northern Party Survived

Meanwhile, any hut would have seemed a luxury to Campbell and his men. In late February, a lengthy blizzard kept them in their tents for more than a week, and by the time it had blown itself out, they realized it was most unlikely that the ship would be able to reach them. They faced the prospect of a winter without shelter, heat, or adequate food. Refusing to allow the situation to defeat him, Campbell decided that they would have to excavate a set

A *view of the main passageway in the ice cave where the men of the Northern Party spent the winter of 1912. They did not leave "the igloo" for months, and this rather depressing view—with light at the end of the tunnel—would have been thrilling compared with the nothingness that surrounded them throughout the darkness of winter.*

The entrance to the ice cave, which was dug with Raymond Priestley's geological axes. This place, referred to by Murray Levick as a "dismal hole," proved to be a life-saving home for the six men of the Northern Party.

of subsurface ice caves. On the face of it, the idea was outlandish, but within several weeks just such a shelter had been cut. It was hacked from the ice and snow covering a granite outcrop that the men named Inexpressible Island.

Their new home, known as "the igloo," was, according to Levick, "a dismal hole." A set of steps led down from a doorway that could be closed off by a sealskin curtain. To one side was a foul latrine, made all the worse by the constipation that the men suffered from because they had virtually no fiber or carbohydrate in their diets. The small passageway included two doorframes made from biscuit cases, and fitted with material to keep out the wind and to help warm the interior. That room was where the six men slept, cooked, ate, and spent their waking hours. It was 12 by 9 feet (3.7 by 2.7 m), with a ceiling so low no one could stand upright. Around the walls were 12-inch- (30-cm-) thick snow blocks placed so as to insulate the room against the ice, which would have drained the heat away more quickly.

On the floor was a covering of gravel and pebbles, above which went dried seaweed, while the top layer was the floorcloth of a tent. Also along the floor, down the center of the room, was an invisible but very real line separating the officers and the men. Always a martinet and a stickler for naval rules, Campbell had designated the side on which the three seamen slept as the mess-deck and the side on which the two officers and the scientist slept as the quarterdeck. "As on board ship," he declared, "everything that is said and done on the mess-deck will be the responsibility of the men and it shall not be heard or paid attention to or interfered with by any of the officers who reside on the quarterdeck. And the opposite is true."

So the six men went about their ordered lives—or as much as they could under the circumstances. Much of their daily existence revolved around food. They had very limited rations left, and Priestley was put in charge of distributing these. Most of their diet, however, consisted of seal and penguin, the killing of which also provided blubber for the small cooking stove that they constructed. The wildlife spent most of its time away from shore, so whenever a seal or penguin did approach, the men immediately tried to dispatch it. One of the most memorable days of the entire, horrible winter was when Browning cut open a seal to find 36 edible fish inside its stomach.

The meat was stored in a small room off the passageway, and one of the more difficult tasks was to cut the hard frozen flesh into pieces small enough to be cooked. Levick reported that to cut up enough seal for two meals could take nearly all day, using a hammer and an iron chisel. The meat and blubber were initially accompanied by only one biscuit per day, although this dropped to no biscuits in August. This dietary regime brought about numerous physical problems, and Browning in particular almost died from the complications.

The cooking of the food had its own ghastly side effects. The blubber that was used for cooking, heating, and to provide a minimum of light once the oil ran low produced a disgusting, greasy, choking pall that hurt the men's eyes and filled the small room with debilitating fumes. It also saturated their clothes with a combination of smoke and oil that, following Browning's West-Country usage, they dubbed "smitch." Once this "smitch" had penetrated clothes or sleeping bags, it ruined the fur and caused it to lose much of its insulating warmth. As it became impregnated in the men's gloves and mitts, they froze hard, so that donning them—an absolutely essential move every time they left the cave—came to be compared to putting on miniature wood boxes.

The cooking and lighting arrangement led to other problems. If placed too close to the wall, the stoves melted the ice. If not enough lights were lit, the inside of the cave became too dark even to read. On May 25, following a blizzard that had helped seal up the front of the cave and the small hole punched in the ceiling to allow some of the fumes to dissipate, the lamps started burning very weakly. Even the primus stove with its oil system would not burn. Only after furious efforts to light the stoves failed did Levick realize that their little domain was running out of oxygen. They made a hole through the new drift, narrowly avoiding what could have been a fatal conclusion.

As spring approached, Campbell began planning the 200-mile (370-km) march that he had decided they would make down the coastline to Hut Point. But in early September, the entire party was stricken with severe enteritis (inflammation of the intestine). By the time they were finally able to leave their igloo on September 30, Dickason and Browning were so weak that the others had to pull the two sledges on their own. The first week, they made less than 30 miles (56 km), and they must have wondered if their goal was even attainable. Progress improved after that, however, and they covered more than double that distance the following week. Slowly they plodded down the coastline, killing a penguin here and there to eat, and on October 29 they arrived at Cape Roberts. Here the Second Western Party had left a cache of food. "It seemed almost too good to be true," Campbell wrote after surveying a store that included two large containers of biscuits and bags of raisins, tea, cocoa, sugar, butter, and lard. They had a "blow out meal" and celebrated by taking the rest of the day off.

The members of the Northern Party after their winter in "the igloo." They left their winter quarters covered with "smitch" and their clothes in tatters. From the left: Petty Officer George Abbott, Commander Victor Campbell, Able Seaman Harry Dickason, geologist Raymond Priestley, Naval Surgeon Murray Levick, and Petty Officer Frank Browning.

As they progressed south during the closing stages of their journey, they came across more depots that had been left by earlier parties, and they slowly began to regain strength, despite the horribly arduous work of hauling the sledges. Then on November 5, they thought they saw other people ahead of them. They were ecstatic. "Priestley and I walked towards them; they apparently stopped," Campbell wrote later. "Priestley started semaphoring while I looked through my glasses. No result. Suddenly they turned and I saw they were Emperor penguins, miraged up in a way that made them look like figures."

Their disappointment over the Emperor penguins was nothing as great as the grief that was to overtake them the next day, however. Reaching Hut Point—which should have been cause for great celebration—they found a message from Atkinson stating that the Polar Party had been lost and that he and a search party had gone south a week earlier to search for their remains. The next day the six men of the Northern Party completed their amazing journey by trekking up to Cape Evans. There they entered an empty hut. It was not long, however, before the geologist Frank Debenham and W. W. Archer, who had replaced Thomas Clissold as the cook for the second year, made an appearance. They were the only two men left at the base. From them the members of the Northern Party began to learn all that had happened during their absence.

Safe at last. The six members of the Northern Party after their arrival at Cape Evans on November 7, 1912, having completed their journey south after perhaps the most harrowing winter in the history of Antarctic exploration. The men (from the left) are Dickason, Abbott, Browning, Campbell, Priestley, and Levick.

The End of a Dream

It had been a sad winter at Cape Evans, with the Polar Party presumed dead, the whereabouts of the Northern Party unknown, and others having left on *Terra Nova*. The command had devolved on Atkinson, who, despite not expecting it, ran a very efficient and egalitarian base. There were only 13 members of the party there that cold, dark winter, but they were united by an already established camaraderie and their continuing scientific efforts, particularly the work carried on by Debenham, Wright, and Nelson.

At Midwinter Atkinson presented the remaining men with the option of trying to discover the fate of Scott and his men or of attempting to relieve Campbell. However, such were the perceived difficulties in reaching the Northern Party, and the hope that the ship would reach them first, that it was agreed they would try to find out what had happened to Scott and the rest of his Polar Party. Atkinson and many of the others thought they had been lost in a crevasse on the Beardmore, but they hoped at least to find a note at one of the depots that would say whether they had indeed reached the Pole. They all agreed that it was of great importance not to leave the record of the expedition incomplete; if they didn't find out what had happened, no one would ever know if Scott's men had reached the Pole, and their effort would have been in vain.

Atkinson's plan was to take 11 men in three parties. Three men, accompanied by the dogs, would travel to the foot of the glacier. The rest would go in two four-man groups, guiding the seven mules that had been brought south the previous autumn on *Terra Nova*. These had been obtained from India on Oates's recommendation.

The members of the mule parties were to ascend as far as the Cloudmaker, a distinctive mountain along the Beardmore Glacier. One party would stop there to collect specimens, while the other would continue to the top of the glacier if necessary. On October 30, the mule party left under the command of Wright, who was a skilled navigator. Accompanying him were Nelson, Gran, Lashly, Crean, Williamson, Keohane, and Hooper. Two days later, Atkinson, Cherry-Garrard, and Demetri followed with the dog teams, soon catching up with and then accompanying the slower-moving mule parties. Steady progress south was made, and on the morning of November 12, some 11 miles (20 km) beyond One Ton Depot, Wright saw what he thought was a cairn and his team veered off toward it. It was a tent.

When the snow was brushed off, Atkinson and Lashly crawled into it. Scott lay between Wilson and Bowers, all three in their sleeping bags where they had died, and Scott's left hand stretched out toward his old friend Wilson. With them were their detailed records, their meteorological log, and the many letters Scott had written at the end.

Scott had left a request that whoever found them was to read his diary and take it home. From it, Atkinson quickly learned the story of what had happened on their quest. He then gathered his friends and read them Scott's "Message to the Public" and the account of Oates's death. Not wanting to take the bodies from the icy tomb that seemed so appropriate, the search party removed the letters and various personal items to return to the families and then took away the bamboo poles, collapsing the tent over the three men. They then built a cairn on top of it, over which they placed a cross, fashioned from skis, in memory of their fallen comrades.

The search party in the spring of 1912. Although the mule party left before the dog teams, they all traveled together for most of the way south. Despite slow progress, in less than two weeks they found the tent that was the final resting place for Scott, Wilson, and Bowers.

Atkinson next led his party south to look for Oates's body, but although they found his sleeping bag, they realized that he had been given a final, mysterious resting place in the snow. Near where his final camp had been, they erected another cairn with a small cross. The sad mission accomplished, Atkinson decided to return to Hut Point and give any help possible to Campbell and the Northern Party. On November 25, the dog teams having pushed ahead of the mules, Atkinson, Cherry-Garrard, and Demetri returned to Hut Point. "Cherry went into the hut," Atkinson later wrote, "and returned with a letter and his face transformed." Campbell and the Northern Party, he had learned, were safe.

On January 18, 1913, *Terra Nova*, under the command of a now-recovered Teddy Evans, arrived at Cape Evans. "Are you all well?" Evans shouted through a megaphone before they landed. After a hushed silence, Campbell, who as the senior officer had taken command on his return, responded, "The Southern Party reached the Pole on January 18 last year, but were all lost on the return journey—we have their records."

Now the men of *Terra Nova* joined their fellows ashore in mourning the loss of the Polar Party, but in celebrating their triumph. Those who had come from New Zealand had already, by now, been made aware of Amundsen's success and his triumphant return. But regardless of success or failure in the attempt to be the first to reach the South Pole, they took consolation in the belief that Scott's party had demonstrated all the qualities that had made the British Empire great.

On January 20, Atkinson led a party to the top of Observation Hill, overlooking both Hut Point and the Great Ice Barrier. There they erected a 9-foot (2.7-m) wood cross as a memorial to Scott and his four comrades, one that still stands today, honoring their valiant struggle and achievements. Cherry-Garrard suggested the last line of Tennyson's "Ulysses" that they inscribed on it: "To strive, to seek, to find and not to yield." Shortly thereafter, the last members of the expedition boarded *Terra Nova* and headed north together, to where their efforts—particularly those of Scott and the Polar Party—would receive international acclaim. Moreover, the triumph, failure, and tragedy that was Scott's expedition would quickly be woven into a great heroic tale that would touch the hearts of the people of the British Empire throughout the world, playing its part as a model of courage and sacrifice that would be evoked again and again in the desperate struggles of two world wars.

The Continuing Debate

In later years, his numerous biographers would present conflicting arguments about Scott's abilities, competence, and genuine success. He has been criticized for the modes of transport he selected, for not establishing One Ton Depot as far south as it should have been, and for being so obsessed with measuring himself against Shackleton's journey as to lose sight of important features of his own.

Blame for the loss of the Polar Party has also been attributed to him, because of his decision to take a fifth man with the final party, his selection of the specific individuals, his changing orders regarding the use of the dogs, and because of his failure to ensure sufficient supplies for the journey home. Each of these criticisms has been explained, to one level or another, in a manner that satisfies those who "support" Scott, but not so completely as to be accepted by his critics. It is a debate that continues today, and it is far from over. But both criticism and excess praise are easy to give in hindsight.

Rather than passing any judgment on him and his handling of his great expedition, perhaps it is better to acknowledge simply that Robert Falcon Scott did do what he said in his final letters that he had done. He did not live, but he did give to the world "a tale to tell of the hardihood, endurance, and courage" of his companions that continues to stir hearts and bring forth emotions wherever, and whenever, it is told.

After the bodies of Scott, Wilson, and Bowers were found, and their letters, journals, and various personal items removed to return to their families, the bamboo poles were taken away, collapsing the tent over the three men. The search party then built a cairn over the icy tomb, on which they placed a cross. There the three men's bodies were left to remain forever in the environment that had played such a role in their lives and deaths.

SELECTED PHOTOGRAPHS

The expedition included 33 Siberian sledge dogs (opposite), which were berthed on the open deck. Scott noted that the animals had the most wretched time, even in calm weather, and they regularly whined pitifully. Waves constantly broke over the bulwarks and drenched them, so that they sat with their coats sodden. One was strangled by his chain in the gale that struck shortly after the expedition sailed south from New Zealand. Another, Osman, was washed overboard by a wave, but was swept right back aboard.
JANUARY 3, 1911

The 19 Manchurian ponies (above) had a miserable journey south in tiny stables located on the upper deck and under the fo'c'sle of Terra Nova—so miserable that some did not complete the voyage. Here, Oates poses with some of his charges, for which he himself had purchased and smuggled aboard five extra tons of fodder.
1910–1912

When Wilfred Bruce *(opposite) was hired for the expedition, his vetting process had undoubtedly taken into account the fact that he was the brother of Scott's wife Kathleen. His first major task was to help Meares bring the ponies and dogs to New Zealand from Siberia. A commander in the Royal Naval Reserve, he was one of the ship's officers, sailing north as winter approached and returning south again the following spring. Besides his regular duties, he kept the zoological log for Lillie during the cruise in March–April 1911.*
1910–1912

Lieutenant Harvey *Rennick (left) wearing an odd combination of fashions aboard* Terra Nova. *Rennick became the executive officer aboard ship once the shore parties had been dropped off.*
1910–1912

Much as cruise-ship passengers doze in the Antarctic sun today, so Terra Nova's crew took advantage of a wind-free, sun-lit corner to nap and read. Space was evidently in short supply.

DECEMBER 1910

Because her heavy supplies put Terra Nova *very low in the water, the pumps often had to be manned in heavy seas. All hands were expected to help, even the officers and* scientific staff. This photograph was taken early in the expedition, as the presence of "Birdie" Bowers on the far left indicates. DECEMBER 1910

The man at the wheel had to say "thank you" twice after this photograph (above) was taken, first to his friend who brought him a warm drink of Oxo and secondly to the photographer. Ponting set up the photograph to please one of the expedition's sponsors, Mr. Maltwood of the Liebig Company, which supplied Oxo and Lemco.
1910–1912

On the last day of November 1910, Wilson recorded in his diary that there was a fair, light wind and that those who were sea sick "really had no reason." By noon on the following day, it was a different story. The barometer was falling and both wind and sea were rising. The wind was so strong that the topgallant sails were taken in, followed by other sails in quick succession; heavy green seas pummeled the overloaded vessel. By Friday, December 2, the steam pumps were unable to keep the stokehold free of water, and the valves became clogged. While Lashly and the leading stokers struggled with them, all hands were called to operate the hand pumps. As can be seen from this picture (opposite), the pumps were deployed in the waist of the ship, and needed to operate continually to prevent Terra Nova from foundering.
MARCH 1912

On December 9,
1910, Terra Nova
entered the pack ice
far north of where a
disappointed Scott
had hoped to meet it
(above). For many of
those aboard it was a
totally new experience,
and they clustered
around the rails of the
fo'c'sle as the ship
progressed into this
new environment.
DECEMBER 9, 1910

As the ship made her
slow way through the
beginning of the closely
packed ice (right),
the scene was one
of incredible splendor.
On December 9,
1910, Scott wrote in
his diary: "The sky
has been wonderful,
with every form of
cloud in every condition
of light and shade; the
sun has continually
appeared through
breaks in the cloudy
heavens from time to
time, brilliantly
illuminating some field
of pack, some steep-
walled berg, or some
patch of bluest sea."
DECEMBER 9, 1910

Norwegian ski
expert Tryggve Gran,
geologist Griffith
Taylor, and physicist
Charles Wright take
a turn as lookouts
in Terra Nova's
maintop (opposite) to
search for open-water
leads in the pack ice.
DECEMBER 22, 1910

Furling the sails on
Terra Nova (above).
A combination of
steam power and wind
was used to maneuver
the ship through the
Antarctic pack ice. The
men aloft are Gran
and Able Seaman
Joseph Leese.
DECEMBER 12, 1910

The ice along the edge
of the land had broken
into large pieces, but
had not been blown out
completely to sea when
Ponting captured this
scene, complete with
inquisitive penguins
doing the exploring
rather than men.
1910–1912

Scientific work was a main priority on Scott's expedition, and meteorological and oceanographic data were collected on a daily basis. Here (right) a water bottle is lowered over Terra Nova's side to assist in oceanographic studies of the temperature and salinity of the Antarctic waters.
DECEMBER 17, 1910

Wilson (right) shot a number of birds and seals for his scientific work. Like all such naturalists, he had to be very careful to make certain he killed his targets, otherwise the injured animals might escape, their deaths not benefiting science. Some of Wilson's specimens are now held in the Natural History Museum in London, where they remain a valuable source of information to biologists.
1910–1912

The officers and scientists in the wardroom of Terra Nova, *which was a large, but somewhat crowded facility. The "ratings" messed separately, in true Royal Navy tradition.*

Scott can be seen at the head of the table, with Wilson two places to the right. Photographs of the King and Queen hang on the wall. 1910–1912

Terra Nova *caught in a band of pack ice (opposite). It took more than 20 days and 61 tons of coal to break through to the open sea beyond the pack.*
DECEMBER 13, 1910

On *December 11, a Sunday, after Scott read Divine Service, all hands left the ship to exercise on the sea ice (above). Some practiced skiing, and Scott professed himself "much pleased" by their efforts.*
DECEMBER 11, 1910

Ponting was intrigued by every aspect of the expedition, in this case the way in which the ship's water supplies were replenished. He later described in The Great White South how "everyone—officers, scientists and men—set-to with a will, taking turns with the picks and shovels, and in a few hours we had shipped ten tons of ice…Thus we replenished our depleted fresh-water supply, and provided an animated scene for the kinematograph."
DECEMBER 11, 1910

Edward Nelson,
Raymond Priestley,
and Frank Debenham
assess the thickness of
an ice floe. Knowledge
of the thickness of the
sea ice covering the sea
surface was important
for safe movement over
the ice between ship
and shore.
DECEMBER 1910

Ponting took this evocative photograph (opposite) of a lone penguin on a craggy floe on Christmas Eve.
DECEMBER 1912

Penguins, seals, and flying birds were shot as zoological specimens either from the ship or from small boats put down in the water (right). Here the "pram" is carefully poled through the ice to reach a few penguins in the distance.
DECEMBER 1910

*S*cott commented on the curious shape of an iceberg in the middle of the pack in his diary on December 20, noting that it had been shaped by tilting and losing some of its top. It was not the only thing trapped in the ice; while the journey south was stalled, men were able to spend a good deal of time off the ship (above). Here, Gran and Able Seaman Thomas McLeod are out on the ice.
DECEMBER 20, 1910

*O*n December 22, while Wilson was busily skinning Adélie penguins for the expedition's Christmas dinner, Ponting took this stunning photograph (right) that captures the play of moonlight across the pack and a glittering stretch of open water.
DECEMBER 22, 1910

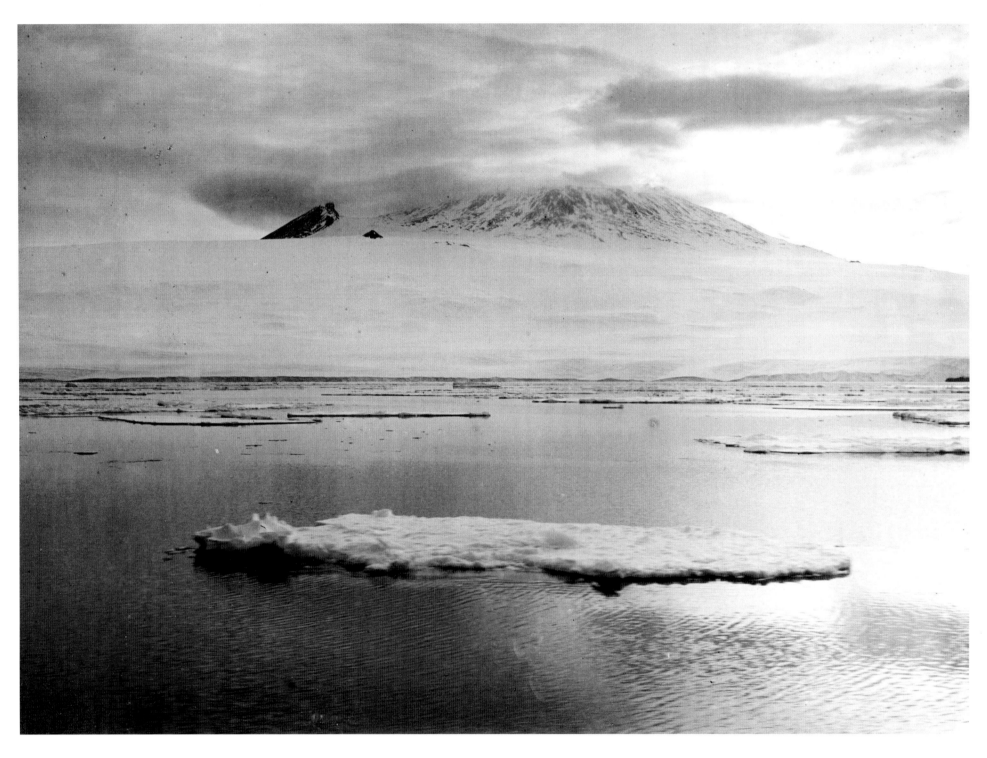

The majestic Mount Erebus (above), with its summit hidden by clouds and smoke, dominates the otherwise placid setting of the shore of Ross Island. Thin wedges of ice float by calmly, in serene comparison to the awsome power of the mighty volcano and the glacial ice. JANUARY 3, 1911

Ponting took this photograph of Mount Erebus (opposite) from Back Door Bay, a small inlet at Cape Royds where Ernest Shackleton had landed much of his equipment. An intricately shaped berg formation makes for an intriguing foreground to the volcano which, Ponting wrote in The Great White South, reminded him of Mount Fuji in Japan. FEBRUARY 16, 1911

In this wonderful
panorama, Ponting
caught the different
kinds of ice that proved
such a challenge to this
and all other Antarctic
expeditions of the time.
1910–1912

Ponting was captivated by the beauty of this grotto (opposite) in the midst of an iceberg. He wrote in The Great White South that it was "the most wonderful place imaginable. From outside, the interior appeared quite white and colourless, but, once inside, it was a lovely symphony of blue and green … by almost incredible good luck, the entrance to the cavern framed a fine view of the Terra Nova lying at the ice-foot." Ponting enthused so wildly about the ice grotto's beauty that several expedition members went to see and admire it. Taylor and Wright are in the grotto here.
JANUARY 5, 1911

Ponting's "most wonderful" grotto (left) was about a mile from the ship, and was the subject of his first photographic excursion in the region of Cape Evans. He took several photographs here, which are among the most famous of his remarkable career. Scott and Wilson both later went with him to see the grotto.
JANUARY 5, 1911

While officers, scientists, and men labored at transporting the expedition supplies from Terra Nova to land, Ponting took photographs, such as these Adélie penguins (above) with the glittering white mass of Mount Erebus looming behind them. This caused some resentment, although Ponting worked long hours and went to endless lengths to secure perfect pictures.
JANUARY 5, 1911

Skuas are fiercely protective of their eggs and young, so the parents of this chick and its unhatched siblings (above) made taking their photograph risky. But Ponting had caught the attention of killer whales during his career, so he probably did not see the skuas as a great danger.
JANUARY 6, 1911

Ponting, wearing his distinctive hat (right), waits with infinite patience for his skua subjects to pose around a seal carcass. Ponting was not the first person to use a cinematograph in the Antarctic—Eric Marshall had done so on Shackleton's British Antarctic Expedition of 1907–09—but the film Ponting made from his footage remains the classic moving picture of early Antarctic exploration.
JANUARY 7, 1911

100

As the unloading process continued on January 7, Ponting managed to capture one remarkable scene after another. Here (left), in one of his most famous photographs, Terra Nova *sits serene and silent in smooth pack ice, while nearer the shore the ice breaks into a jumble of crags and jetties reflected in frigid pools.*
JANUARY 7, 1911

On January 8, *it was decided that* Terra Nova *was too vulnerable so close to the shore, so she was moved a mile away to a safer anchorage. This meant a much longer walk across the pack ice to unload supplies. Here (above), Scott, Wilson, and Teddy Evans make the tedious journey back.*
JANUARY 9, 1911

One problem with taking ponies to the Antarctic was the amount of bulky feed they required. Bales of fodder were placed on sledges (above) and then man-hauled across the sea ice to the hut and stables. Man-hauling was something Scott was very good at, and he doubtless saw the entire landing operation as an excellent chance for the men to become accustomed to doing it.
JANUARY 1911

On January 8, 1911, Teddy Evans noted in his diary with typical British understatement: "This morning a regrettable accident took place... [right] The third and newest motor sledge was hoisted out and, while being hauled clear on to the firm ice, it broke through and sank in deep water... It was nobody's fault, as Simpson and Campbell both tested the floe first and found it quite thick and apparently good. However, there it is, in about 100 fathoms of water."
JANUARY 8, 1911

Until the expedition's hut was built, the most luxurious retreat at Cape Evans was a large green canvas tent (opposite). In this picture, several of the men enjoy their lunch during a brief respite from the arduous tasks of unloading the ship and building their more permanent winter quarters.
JANUARY 7, 1911

Terra Nova's leading shipwright, Francis Davies, shown working on the hut (left), was the key figure in constructing what would be home for the members of the expedition in the months ahead. With some enthusiasm, Scott wrote in his diary that, "all agree that [the hut] should be the most perfectly comfortable habitation… The sides have double boarding inside and outside the frames, with a layer of our excellent quilted seaweed insulation between each layer of boardings… To add to the wall insulation, the south and east sides of the hut are piled high with compressed forage bales."
JANUARY 10, 1911

The hut was a remarkably large and well-built structure. Two of the men involved in making sure it would be a safe and comfortable place to live were Petty Officers Robert Forde and George Abbott (left). Abbott would soon be helping construct another hut at Cape Adare, as a member of the expedition's Northern Party.
JANUARY 10, 1911

Terra Nova *lies calmly at the ice foot late in the unloading process. Several days later, the hut was proclaimed habitable, and soon after that, depot parties began making their way south. Meanwhile, the ship was prepared to take the Eastern Party to King Edward VII Land where, as it later transpired, it was unable to land the party due to heavy ice.*
JANUARY 15, 1911

Early during their stay on Ross Island, two men, a sledge, and their dog team pause with an unobstructed view of mighty Mount Erebus. The characteristic plume of smoke and steam easing from the top of the active volcano is carried off to the right by the Antarctic wind.
JANUARY 15, 1911

Behind the hut, a gravelly slope rises sharply to a rocky peak called *Wind Vane Hill*. Today, it bears a cross that is a memorial to several men who died on Shackleton's Ross Sea Party, but in 1911 it was where Simpson installed some of his meteorological equipment (left). Measurements of temperature and wind speed and direction were taken every day, even when conditions were atrocious.
MARCH 1911

As the season advanced and the sun dipped lower and lower in the sky, work continued on the hut, which was to be the party's winter refuge (right). It was important to ensure that the building, in particular the roof, and the supplies were as wind- and weather-resistant as possible to withstand gales and blizzards. The fact that the hut still stands at the beginning of the 21st century is a testament to the skills of those who built it.
MARCH 26, 1911

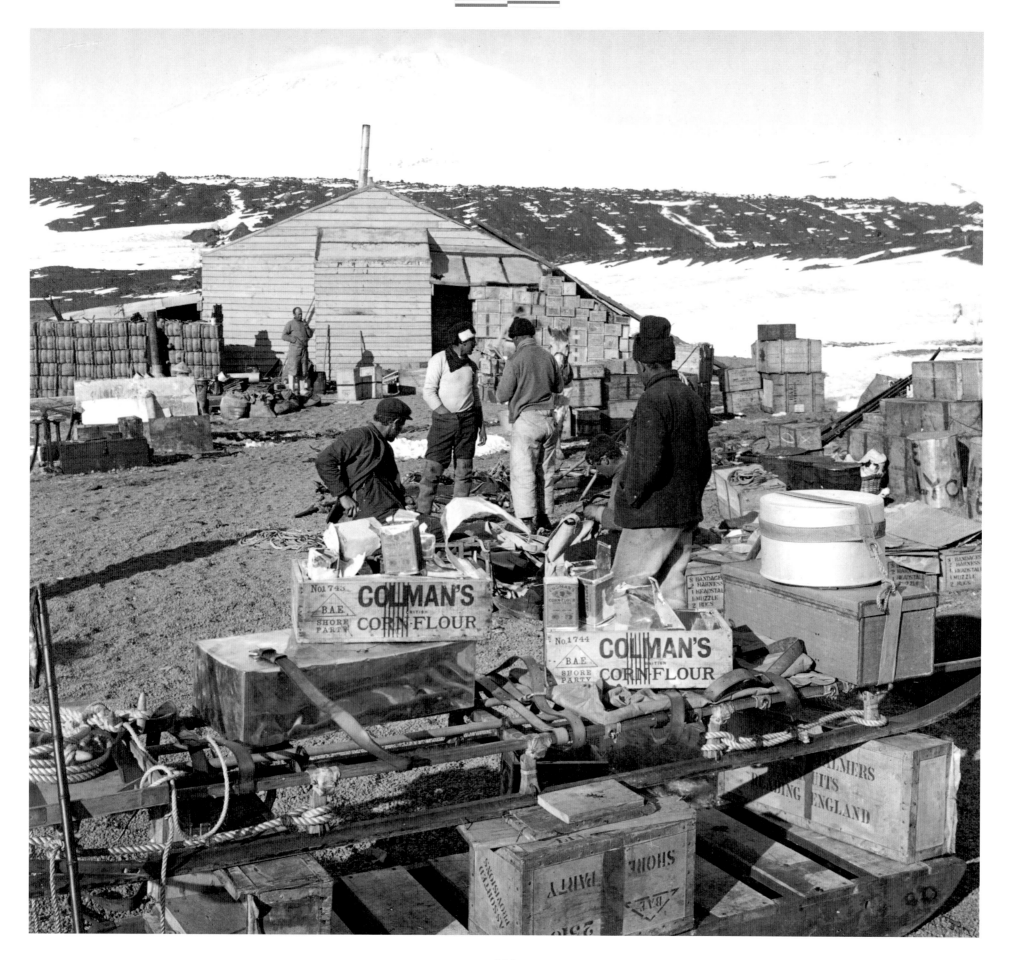

Laying depots, such as this one (right), was an important part of late summer and fall activities, and began as January waned. Supplies were cached for the various journeys that were planned for the following year. This depot, carefully marked by a dark flag, included large amounts of biscuits provided by one of the expedition's major sponsors, Huntley & Palmer.
FEBRUARY 8, 1911

For several weeks after landing, the site of the winter quarters was one of ordered chaos. Vast quantities of food, fuel, sledging rations, scientific equipment, and other material had to be organized and stored. As seen in the photograph (opposite), Colman's of Norwich was one of the expedition's sponsors. Containers bearing the company's name can still be seen in the hut, which is overseen by the New Zealand authorities.
JANUARY 23, 1911

This photograph (left) was one of many taken by Ponting to gratify a sponsor, in this case, Colman's of Norwich, which provided the corn flour being used by this sledging party as well as a large quantity of mustard. Also seen in the photograph is some of the new sledging wear, consisting of a vest and drawers, woollen shirt, jersey, balaclava, wind suit, two pairs of socks, and ski boots.
FEBRUARY 7, 1911

Scott was pleased to have F. J. Hooper (opposite) as a member of the shore party, noting that the former Royal Navy steward would be able to free the scientists from the "dirty work" of daily camp chores. Hooper also played an active role in the motor sledge party at the beginning of the Southern Journey. To judge from this photograph, one of his other duties was to pose with some of the expedition supplies in order for Ponting to take publicity shots for sponsors. Here he fulfils the expedition obligations to Messrs. Heinz & Co.
1910–1912

At one stage, two ponies were lowered from Terra Nova into the Sound and forced to swim ashore, towed by a boat. In an effort to warm up the shivering creatures, the men tried to give them whisky (above). Since Scott deemed the ponies essential for the attempt on the Pole, all hands were determined to save this one, who obviously had little interest in imbibing.
FEBRUARY 8, 1911

Surgeon Murray Levick (in his rabbit hat) was the man who eventually succeeded in pouring the fiery brew down the reluctant horse's throat (right). Unfortunately, although one pony soon seemed fine, the other never fully recovered from its dunking and had to be put down.
FEBRUARY 8, 1911

In January 1911, Ponting took a number of photos of Terra Nova *tied to the ice foot and near an exquisite iceberg. Not published previously, this panorama of the scene gives broader* detail than any of the other photos of the series, and shows how truly small the ship and her crew were compared to their physical surroundings. 1910–1912

116

Besides photographs, Ponting also took moving pictures with his cinematograph as a permanent record of the expedition. He described in some detail the difficulties of using his equipment in conditions of extreme cold, mostly because it involved him removing his fur mittens. This photograph (right) appears to have been one of Ponting's favorite pictures of himself at work.
1910–1912

Terra Nova *framed by the edge of a berg at the ice foot (opposite).*
JANUARY 16, 1911

As the support party returned from the Barrier, Ponting caught on camera the weariness and relief that showed on each of their faces. The three men here (from the left) are the motor mechanic Bernard Day and the steward F. J. Hooper, who were the first two men to return from the south, and Demetri, who came back with a dog team from the base of the Beardmore Glacier. Note the lighter skin around their eyes, protected from the elements by their goggles.
DECEMBER 1911–
JANUARY 1912

Three more members of the support party upon their return to Cape Evans from helping the Polar Party. They are (from the left) Cecil Meares, whose subsequent departure on Terra Nova left an unfilled gap in the level of experience among the expedition members in driving and handling the dog teams; Petty Officer Keohane; and Cherry-Garrard, whom Scott had told that it had been a "toss up" whether he or Oates should continue.
JANUARY 1912

On December 22, having established the Upper Glacier Depot, four of the remaining dozen men were "told off" by Scott and returned to base. Of these, Charles "Silas" Wright, the Canadian physicist, was perhaps the most disappointed, "rather bitterly, I fear," according to Scott. This photograph was taken on his return to Cape Evans in late January 1912.

JANUARY 29, 1912

On April 13, 1911, Scott, photographed here by Ponting, returned to Cape Evans with two parties of his men from a period spent at Hut Point after having been cut off from their main base by the sea ice blowing out of McMurdo Sound.
APRIL 13, 1911

122

*O*ther members of the shore party, who had been forced to remain for weeks at Hut Point in the fall of 1911 while the sea ice refroze on McMurdo Sound, photographed by Ponting. Clockwise (from top left) are Wilson, physicist "Silas" Wright, Tryggve Gran, and Second-in-Command Teddy Evans.
APRIL 1911

One of the men who returned with Scott to Cape Evans was Griffith Taylor (left), an Australian geologist who had been in command of the First Western Party. Like his colleague Frank Debenham, Taylor was a former student of T. W. Edgeworth David, one of the most influential figures in early Antarctic geology.
APRIL 13, 1911

Two other expedition members who returned to Cape Evans on April 13 were the petty officers, Edgar Evans and Tom Crean (opposite).
APRIL 13, 1911

Taken with a telephoto lens from 70 miles (130 km) away—right across McMurdo Sound—this photograph shows the outline of Mount Lister as well as the smaller peaks in front of it. Ponting also managed to catch in his frame the dying iceberg in the foreground. The berg has grounded, and tides and waves are eroding its base.
FEBRUARY 10, 1911

When the water surface was frozen (opposite), members of the expedition marveled at the eerily silent sea's edge. However, when the shore was ice free (above), waves pounded the beaches, smashing the ice into small pieces and breaking over the larger floes. The rounded edges of the ice demonstrate the weathering action of the waves. FEBRUARY 28, 1911

Antarctic ice in various forms. Sastrugi (wind-blown ridges or dunes in the snow) on the Barne Glacier (right); this made the surface rough and sledge travel extremely difficult. Pancake ice (far right) is produced when small floes of slush or grease ice form plates that gently rub up against each other so that the soft edges are pushed upward slightly. This form of sea ice was the beginning of that which prevented Pennell and Terra Nova from relieving the Northern Party in the summer and autumn of 1912.
FEBRUARY 1911– DECEMBER 1912

Young ice forming close to the land's edge (right). The sea surface looks greasy; hence the term "grease ice." The heavy ice furrows photographed at Cape Evans after a blizzard (far right) made even walking around camp unpleasantly difficult.
MARCH 7–8, 1911

Pancake ice (opposite) is thin, rounded cakes with raised rims that form in gently moving seas. It is an early form of sea ice and marks the beginning of the freezing of the waters.
MARCH 15, 1911

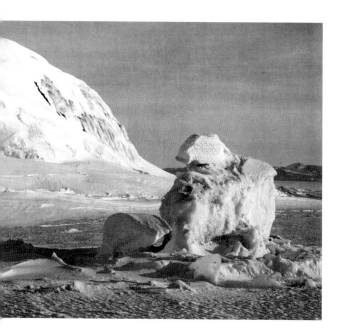

In early November 1911, Ponting took this stunning photograph (above) dominated by Ross Island.
NOVEMBER 4, 1911

Mount Erebus, shown surrounded by a lenticular cloud, dominates the views east from McMurdo Sound and the landing sites along it. The glacier ice flowing down to the water's edge at West Beach made the area lovely but difficult to reach.

MARCH 7, 1911

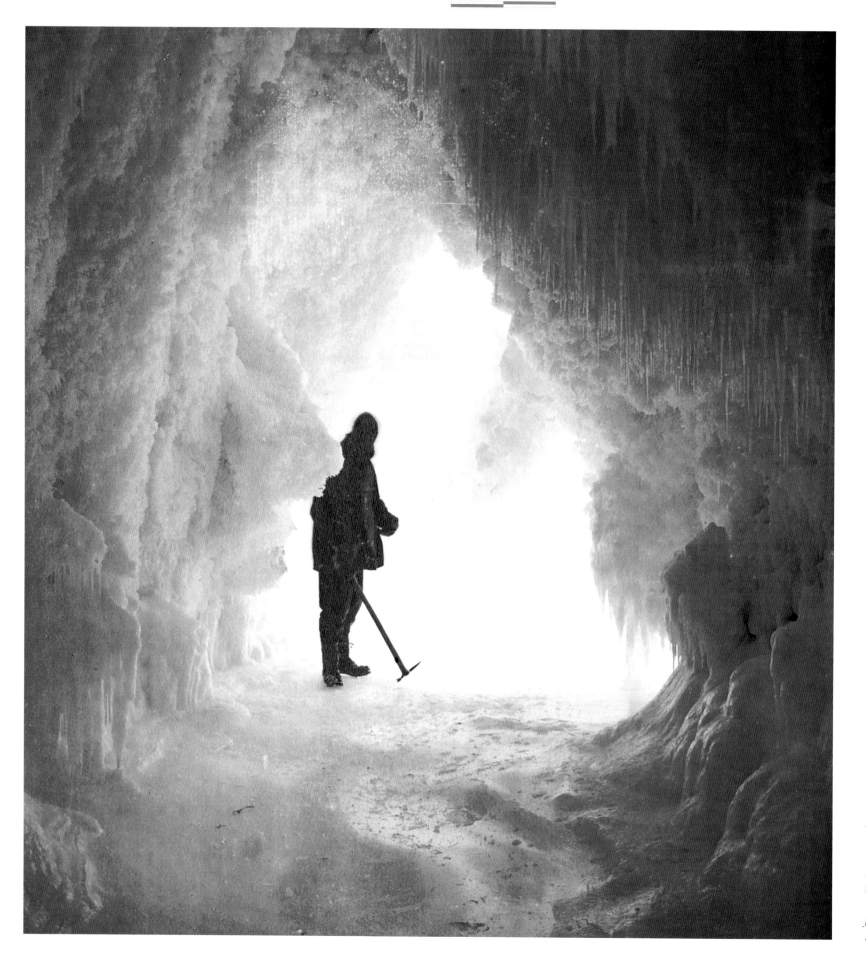

As winter approached, Scott wrote, "I came back with the impression that we should not find our winter walks so interesting as those at Hut Point, but I'm rapidly altering my opinion." One of the places that helped change his mind was this ice cave (left) in Land's End Glacier, where Scott can be seen with his ice axe.
APRIL 28, 1911

Once he began exploring the area around Cape Evans, Scott became excited about its natural beauty (opposite). On April 28, he recorded in his diary: "Went to ice caves on glacier S. of Cape; these are really wonderful. Ponting took some photographs with long exposure and Wright got some very fine ice crystals."
APRIL 28, 1911

*C*ape Evans had a serene, beautiful look at times, although it was much less so during the harsh winter Scott's party was to spend there. Here Ponting caught the sunlight reflecting off the water. Near the hut are many different depots of supplies and gear, which were placed wide apart to avoid the risk of fire.
1910–1912

Home for the men
(opposite). Drifted
snow covers the
supplies in the fore-
ground, while the heat
of the stoves inside the
hut keeps the roof
relatively clear. Skis
were always set upright
so they would not be
lost in drifted snow.
JUNE 13, 1911

Scientific observations
went on all winter and
Ponting was keen to
capture as many
activities as possible
with his lens.
Lieutenant Evans
(above) was one of
his victims, forced to
pose in sub-zero
temperatures until
Ponting was satisfied
with the result. Evans
was viewing an
occultation of Jupiter
and he was in
telephone contact with
Dr. Simpson inside the
hut, who was timing
the observation.
JUNE 8, 1911

Throughout the winter the ponies (above) were cared for with remarkable tenderness by Oates, who had a deep affection for them even if he considered them to be of a lower quality than he would have chosen himself. In the early winter, it was already so cold that the ponies' breath condensed while Oates stood with them in companionable silence.
MAY 25, 1911

Next to the main body of the hut were the stables where the ponies were kept throughout the winter of 1911 (right). In this area was a stove that burned seal blubber rather than traditional fuel, which was saved for the main hut and for the journeys to the interior. Here, Meares and Oates sit contentedly smoking their pipes adding to the already smoky atmosphere.
MAY 26, 1911

One thing the dark and cold of winter could not interfere with was the expedition's scientific program. Here (right) the two geologists with the main party at Cape Evans—Frank Debenham and Griffith Taylor— carefully engage in their scientific work.
MAY 22, 1911

Throughout the long, dark winter of 1911, the members of the expedition attempted to repair and improve the equipment they had brought with them, based on their experiences on the Barrier in January and February 1911. One of their most important tasks was mending their heavy sleeping bags. Here (opposite) two petty officers, Crean and Evans, are sewing the reindeer-skin sleeping bags.
MAY 16, 1911

Like many Royal Navy officers, Lieutenant Evans (left) had training in drafting and map-making. This allowed him to make a continuing contribution to the expedition throughout the winter.
MAY 23, 1911

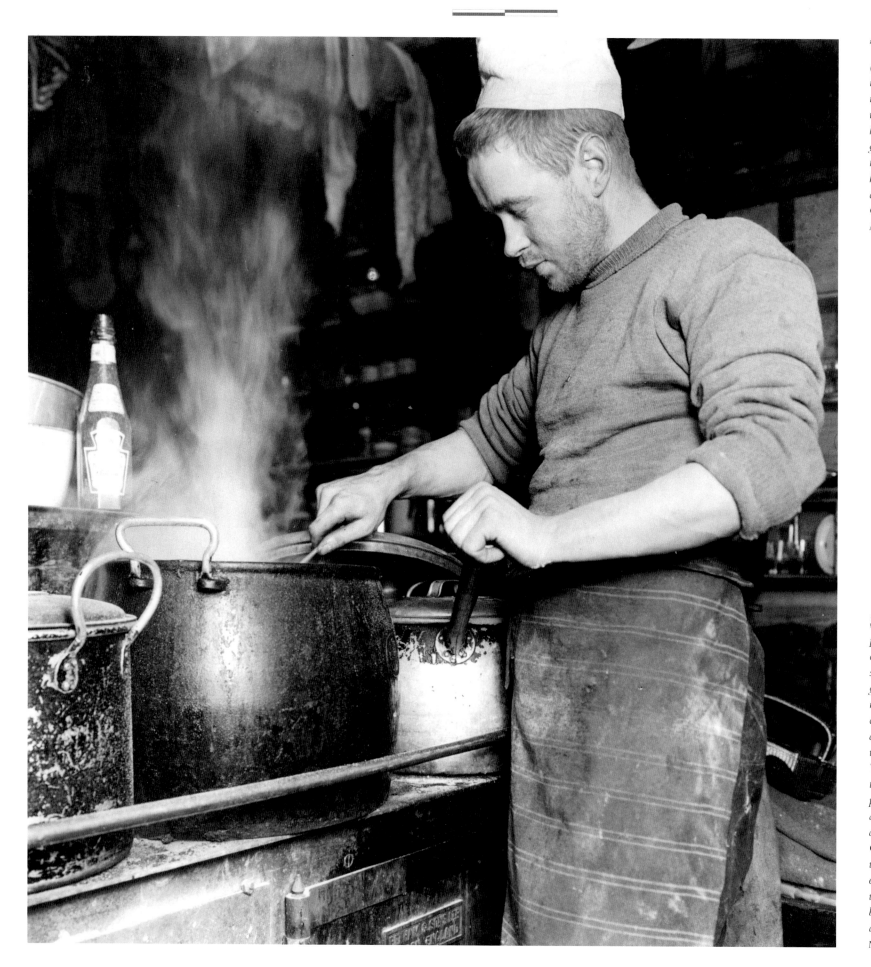

Thomas Clissold (left) producing a meal in the galley. His job usually meant that he was the last man to have to worry about getting too cold. Note the Heinz tomato ketchup with its distinctive label behind Clissold's pan.
AUGUST 30, 1911

Scott had faced major problems with the cook on his first expedition, so this time he went to great lengths to find a man who would not only be an excellent cook, but would fit in with the expedition. Thomas Clissold fit the bill, and was popular as well as appreciated for his culinary skills. Among Clissold's many jobs was to keep the expedition members well supplied with fresh bread, which he baked daily (opposite).
MARCH 26, 1911

One of the most
important sets of
equipment brought
south was the
thermometers. They
came in a variety of
types and had several
uses, both for
observations at base

and for data collection
by the different parties
in the field. In the
photograph (opposite),
they are being tested
for accuracy.
JULY 14, 1911

Dr. Atkinson (above)
in the small laboratory
used for the biological
and parasitological
research. Atkinson was
not only one of the
scientific staff, but was
also the surgeon at the
main base and, after
his return with the

support team to
the Polar Party, the
commanding officer
at Cape Evans. The
wealth of equipment
indicates the seriousness
with which Scott took
the expedition's
scientific program.
SEPTEMBER 15, 1911

Bowers, Atkinson, and Cherry-Garrard (above) cut up and measure the stores of pre-produced pemmican for the spring and summer sledging journeys. Each portion was weighed carefully to make certain all rations were identical.
JUNE 23, 1911

On June 6, 1911, the expedition members celebrated their leader's 43rd birthday. The hut was decorated with the sledging flags of each of the inhabitants (opposite). The party included, from left, Oates (standing), Meares, Cherry-Garrard, Taylor, Nelson, Evans, Scott, Wilson, Simpson, Bowers, Gran (standing), Wright, and Debenham. The hands of Atkinson (to the left) and Day (to the right) are also in the photograph.
JUNE 6, 1911

*Some geological
specimens needed to
be polished before they
could be examined
microscopically
(opposite). Frank
Debenham, well
wrapped up against
the chill even inside the
hut, prepares samples.*
JULY 12, 1911

*Scott was a great
enthusiast about
modern technology,
and he had a telephone
cable run all the way
from Cape Evans to
Hut Point (right),
making use of the
new contraption for
communication about
scientific observations.
Shortly before he left on
the Southern Journey,
he noted in his diary,
"This morning
Simpson has just rang
up. He says the motors
are in difficulties with
the surface. The trouble
is just that which I
noted as alarming on
Monday—the chains
slip on the very light
covering of hard ice."*
JULY 14, 1911

As on Scott's first expedition, an in-house magazine entitled The South Polar Times was produced by this expedition. Cherry-Garrard (above) was editor, following in the footsteps of Shackleton, who had been so on the Discovery Expedition almost a decade before. Day

bound the volume in a cover of venesta wood and sealskin. The first issue, released on Midwinter's Day, included a geological article by Taylor and a plan of the forthcoming Southern Journey by Scott, as well as poems and lighter, more humorous pieces.
AUGUST 30, 1911

One of the most impressive tasks performed during the winter at Cape Evans was masterminded by Petty Officer Patrick Keohane. He is shown (opposite) putting the final touches to his accurately proportioned and extremely intricate model of Terra Nova.
AUGUST 10, 1911

Petty Officer Evans is often remembered for his remarkable physical strength and ability. However, he was a man of many talents, as shown by his work (opposite) at the sewing machine in overhauling the sleeping bags and canvas tents for the Polar Party.
1910–1912

Dr. George Simpson (above) had tried unsuccessfully to join Scott's first expedition. His quality as a scientist was proved beyond a shadow of a doubt on this venture, as he made a series of meteorological observations that are still used as a basis of comparison today. Here he is at work in the hut where magnetic data were recorded.
JANUARY 5, 1912

The "tenements" (left) were a chaotic cluster of five bunk beds and belongings that were home to Cherry-Garrard (left), Bowers (standing), Oates (middle), Meares (top right), and Atkinson (bottom right). The scene can still be viewed in Scott's hut, with socks drying at the end of the bed and harnesses hanging in a jumble, almost as if their owners had "just gone outside" and are expected to return soon.
OCTOBER 9, 1911

Ponting gave several winter lectures, including one on his photographic work in Japan (above), using glass slides from his book In Lotus-Land: Japan. *As Scott wrote in his diary, "To-night Ponting gave us a charming lecture on Japan with wonderful illustrations of his own. He is happiest in his descriptions of the artistic side of the people, with which he is in fullest sympathy. So he took us to see the flower pageants… His descriptions were well given and we all of us thoroughly enjoyed our evening."*
OCTOBER 16, 1911

Captain Scott spent a good deal of his time in the small den he used as an office and bedroom (opposite). In it he wrote reports, made plans for the forthcoming attempt on the Pole and penned the diaries published after his death as Scott's Last Expedition. *Ponting was proud of this photograph, and felt* he had captured something of the leader in it. It is easily one of the most famous pictures of Scott.
OCTOBER 7, 1911

Sledges lie basking in the sunlight (above), ready for summer journeys. The cirrus clouds are an indication of fine weather to come, and the glacier at the rear gleams brilliantly in the dazzling light.
DECEMBER 19, 1911

Man-hauling was not an enjoyable pastime, so posing for Ponting whilst in full harness would have been a welcome respite. 1910–1912

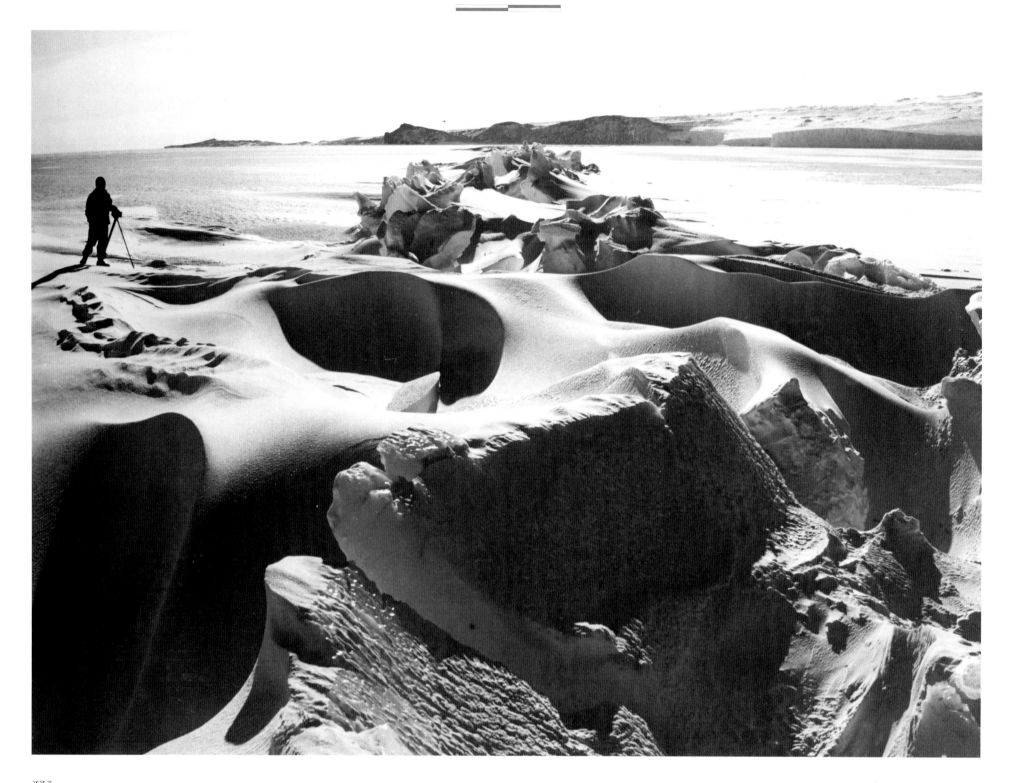

Where sea ice comes under pressure, ridges may develop as floes are forced over one another. Shown (above) is the pressure ridge formed between Barne Glacier and Inaccessible Island.
OCTOBER 8, 1911

In October 1911, Ponting found this curiously weathered iceberg (opposite) in South Bay, with Mount Erebus smoking gently in the background.
OCTOBER 8, 1911

162

Surveying and map-making was chilly work, and no one liked spending additional time at the plane table while Ponting fiddled with his lenses and buttons. Debenham (left and below) does not manage a smile as he poses in September 1911.
SEPTEMBER 9, 1911

Ponting named the ice formation (right) "Castle Berg." He persuaded Clissold to pose for him, but at one point, the cook fell and suffered a concussion, giving the photographer a considerable fright. The injury sustained was serious enough to prevent Clissold from accompanying the motor party on the early stage of the Southern Journey.
SEPTEMBER 17, 1911

164

Ponting couldn't get enough of Castle Berg (opposite). In The Great White South he wrote that in the sunlight, "the berg became of such gleaming beauty that even the most unimpressionable members of our community felt the influence of its spell. There was but one opinion concerning it amongst us—that it was the most wonderful iceberg ever reported in the Polar regions." SEPTEMBER 17, 1911

Another view of Castle Berg (above), this time taken by flashlight in June 1911, the middle of winter. Ponting masterfully captures the darkness and shadows, which set it off in a mysterious and captivating manner. JUNE 4, 1911

Scott, in the center of the photograph, and other expedition members prepare for their departure on an early stage of the Southern Journey. Ponting accompanied his colleagues as far as the Great Ice Barrier, where he said what proved to be a final farewell to Scott and the other four members of the final Polar Party.
1910–1912

The members of the Second Western Party had been waiting for nearly a month to be picked up by Terra Nova *when they finally saw the ship. They began to race toward her (right), attempting to pull their sledge across some two miles (3.7 km) of cracking ice floes. Four men came out to meet the party and helped haul the sledge over the floes, which were rapidly breaking up and floating northward in great fragments. When their way was slowed by the increasing distance between the floes, the ship butted a large floe toward the ice they were on and held it there long enough for the men to get the sledge across to safety. This photograph shows the party gathering speed to propel their sledge across a gap between floes.*
MARCH 1911

At the start of the Southern Journey, Day's motor sledge passes Inaccessible Island (above and top). Teddy Evans, who was in command of the motor sledges, guides Day's sledge through some difficult terrain.
NOVEMBER 1911

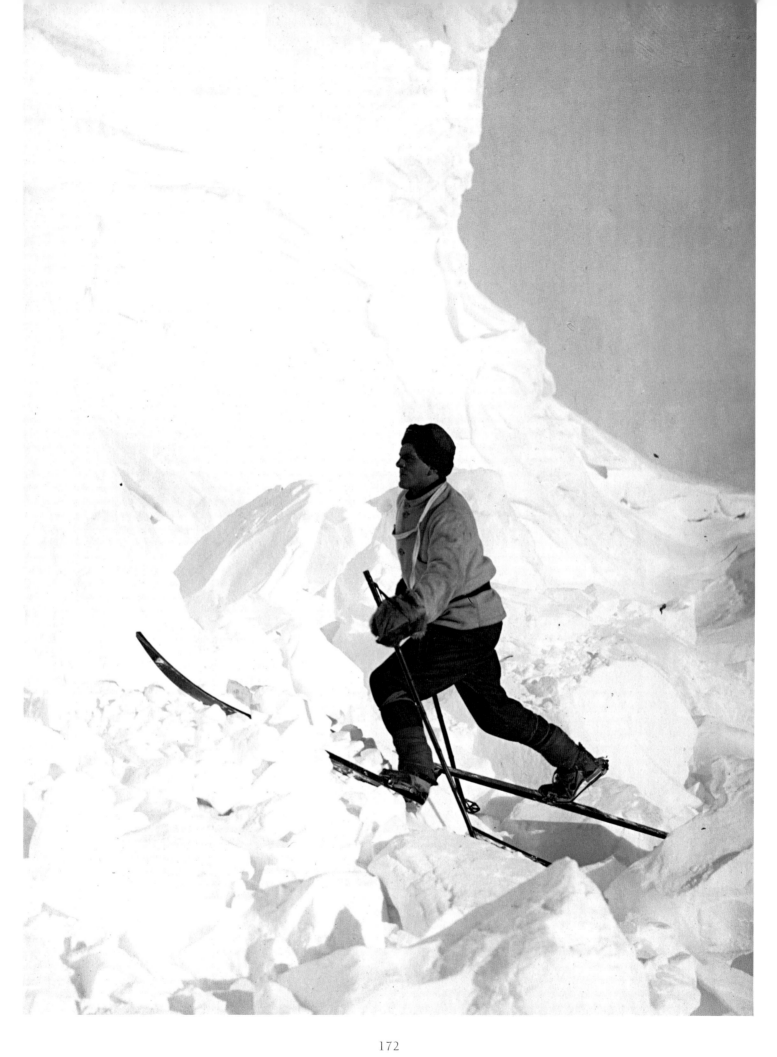

Scott hired Tryggve Gran at the urging of Fridtjof Nansen after the young Norwegian put on an impressive display of his skiing ability while Scott was testing the motor sledges in Norway. As shown here (opposite), Gran had the ability to move well in all conditions of ice and snow, including hauling a sledge. Although some expedition members improved greatly from Gran's instructions, not all of the men made the necessary efforts to learn how to ski properly.
OCTOBER 1911

Ponting had a remarkable talent for being able to find just the right angle and perspective for his photographs—even standing on his head (right), if he thought it necessary.
JANUARY 1912

Although some of the scientists on the expedition, such as Atkinson and Wright, were important members of the support party, others took advantage of the long daylight hours of summer to conduct scientific research while the main body of the expedition was engaged with the Southern Journey. One of those left at Cape Evans was Nelson, the biologist. He demonstrates in these photographs (this page and opposite) the method of collecting water samples from below the sea ice with his mobile winch, which was attached to a Nansen-Petersen insulated water bottle.
DECEMBER 24, 1911

Nelson winding his winch to bring up biological samples from the water below the ice (left). Nelson and the meteorologist "Sunny Jim" Simpson were the two scientists left at Cape Evans throughout the summer sledging season.
DECEMBER 24, 1911

A close-up (left) of the winch that was used to bring up biological samples from the water below the ice.
DECEMBER 24, 1911

Each expedition
member tended to work
with his "own" pony
in order to learn the
animal's eccentricities
and how to get the best
from it. Wilson's pony
was Nobby (above)
and Cherry-Garrard
led Michael (opposite).
The ponies loved to
roll in the snow,
probably to relieve the
itching on their skin.

These photographs
were taken when the
ponies were being
broken in by the men
to the realities of
dragging sledges.
OCTOBER 1911

Clissold and Anton
Omelchenko torment
an Emperor penguin
that had the misfortune
to wander into their
hands (above).
1910–1912

Ponting was delighted
when he found this
Adélie penguin rookery
placed artistically before
Mount Erebus (right).
Sometimes thought
of as the "classic"
penguin, Adélies are
found in large numbers
around much of the
Antarctic continent.
This particular rookery
is at Cape Royds.
NOVEMBER 27, 1911

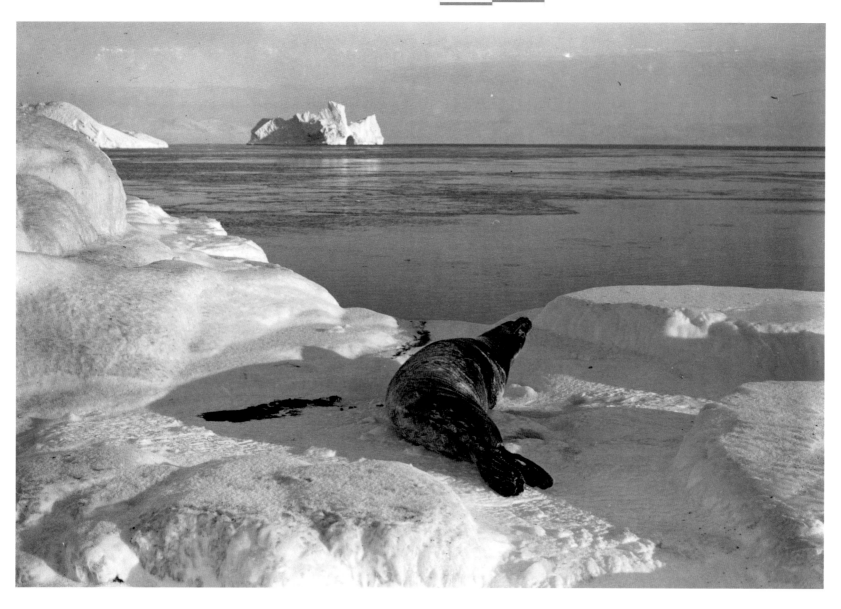

A skua lands next to a dead penguin to feed (opposite). Skuas are predators and scavengers, as happy taking fresh prey such as penguin chicks as they are feasting on a corpse. Skuas are careful not to take on adult penguins, which have powerful beaks and wings. Any injury that prevents a skua from flying will almost certainly result in its death, particularly if it cannot fly north at the end of the summer. Behind the birds, the ponies, tethered to each other to prevent them from running away, nose the snow in a futile hunt for a blade of grass below it. 1910–1912

Weddell seals (above and right) are true Antarctic mammals in that they remain far south even when the sea is covered in ice. They do, however, need access to leads, polynias, or breathing holes in order to come up for air. Weddell seals make breathing holes by gouging the ice from below with their strong and very hard teeth. The sharp, grating sound of enamel on rock-hard ice is a common sound near these holes in winter, as the seals' survival often depends on keeping them from freezing over. Such activities are hard on their teeth, which gradually wear down to gum level. When a seal reaches the point where it can no longer keep its holes open, it may well drown, a process known as "dental death." 1910–1912

Hooper and Demetri join several seals on the ice. This was most likely not a social visit; seals hauled out conveniently near to the base or the ship were usually killed to provide a supply of fresh meat for the party throughout the winter. 1910–1912

Scott expressed reservations about the use of dogs on the Southern Journey, although he knew that Amundsen planned to use them. Part of the problem was a lack of understanding among most British explorers about the animals, their diet, and how to train and drive them. This meant that the dogs Scott had taken on his previous expedition had performed poorly. Moreover, like many Britons, Scott felt an empathy with animals, and disliked seeing their misery as their health and spirits failed. Meares showed Scott how effective dogs could be in the Antarctic, but by the time Scott realized this, it was too late to use them. The four expedition dogs here are: Kasoi (top left), Trésor (top right), Ostrenos (bottom left), and Mannike Noogis (bottom right).
1910–1912

Four more of the dogs used during Scott's expedition. They are: Biela Noogis (top left), Cook (top right), Vaida (bottom left), and Osman (bottom right). Schools in Britain contributed funds for Meares's purchase of the dogs in Siberia. Although each school named the dog that it was credited with giving to the expedition, the dogs, needless to say, continued to respond to the Russian names they had already been given in Siberia.
1910–1912

Three more dogs used during the expedition . They are: Krisravitsa (top left), Bieleglas (top right), and Stareek (bottom). Wilson was patient with the dog teams, despite having trouble controlling them once they had caught wind of a seal—and there were plenty hauled out around the coast. Wilson wrote in his diary on January 30, 1911 that "Dog driving like this in the orthodox [that is, Russian] manner is a very different thing to the beastly dog driving we perpetrated in the Discovery days. I got to love all my team and they got to know me well, and my old leader even now—I am writing this six months after I have had anything to do with any of them—never fails to come and speak to me whenever he sees me, and he knows me and my voice ever so far off. He is quite a ridiculous 'old man' [Stareek means Old Man in Russian] and quite the nicest, quietest, cleverest old dog gentleman I have ever come across. He looks in face as if he knew all the wickedness of all the world and all its cares and as though he was bored to death by both of them."
1910–1912

Weddell seals basking on pancake ice in the sea off Cape Evans (opposite). Weddells, like Crabeater and Leopard seals, are often seen hauled out on ice floes; Southern Elephant seals and Antarctic fur seals are more often seen on beaches. During the moulting season, when they shed their fur, Weddell seals may gather in groups of hundreds of animals. Unlike Southern Elephant seals, which lie in large piles to conserve body heat, Weddell seals do not touch each other when they moult.
1910–1912

Seals hauled out at the foot of the towering Church Berg. Some larger icebergs were semi-permanent features of the expedition's landscape, having become trapped in winter sea ice and, sometimes, aground in shallow water.
DECEMBER 29, 1911

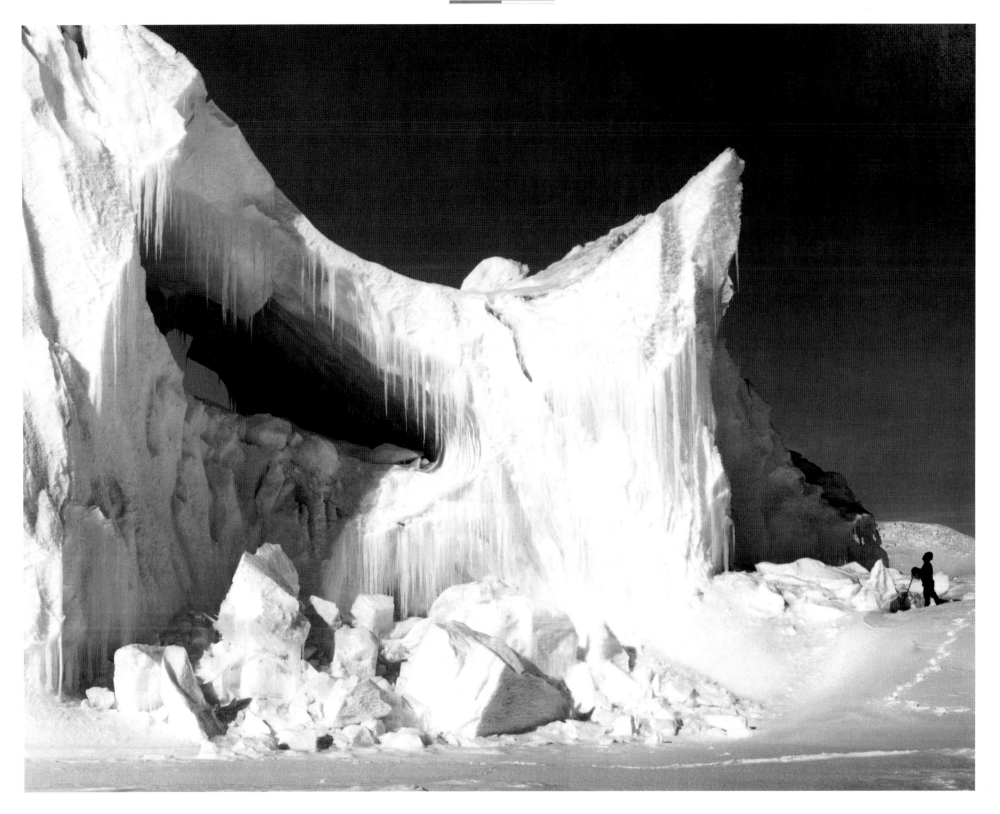

"The warm [sun], beating on [icebergs], melted [the] snow, so that white ice only remained, tinged with the delicate hues of aquamarine and tourmaline; whilst every crack was turquoise and each deeper fissure azure," wrote Ponting in The Great White South. DECEMBER 29, 1911

189

Ponting was always looking for the unusual, and he clearly caught it with this breathtaking scene (left) of the effect of the Sun through clouds on the ice at Cape Royds. NOVEMBER 27, 1911

In a land of ice and snow, the pillar at Cape Barne (above) stands out in striking fashion. Cape Barne was one of Ponting's favorite photographic areas, but usually the emphasis of his photography was on the great icy cape itself, rather than the bits of earth nearby. NOVEMBER 29, 1911

An anticipated arrival or a fond farewell? Ponting turned this scene with the ship, four lone men on shore, and the boat into a haunting shot emphasizing the shore party's physical and mental distance from civilization. Cape Barne is seen to the right-hand side.
1910–1912

193

Terra Nova *berthed alongside the pack ice at Butter Point (right), ready to collect the Western Party in February 1912. The task of the Western Party, which consisted of Taylor, Debenham, Gran, and Petty Officer Robert Forde, had been to conduct a geological survey near Granite Harbour in the "Western Mountains" of South Victoria Land.*
1912

Biologist *Dennis Lillie (opposite) displays some of the siliceous sponges he collected by dredging the ocean bottom. Lillie spent the entire expedition aboard* Terra Nova *and gathered a remarkable collection of specimens.*
1912

Tabular *icebergs (right) are flat-topped pieces of glacier ice with straight-sided cliffs. They calve from the great ice shelves and are made up of snowfall-derived fresh water. The largest of these mammoths can be tens of miles long and several hundred yards thick.*
1912

The Ship's Crew

After spending the winter in warmer climes, Terra Nova returned to the Antarctic in January 1912, bringing supplies, a passage home for some of those who had wintered, and replacements for some of the staff.
1912

The men in the front row of this photograph (above), taken on the return to New Zealand, are (from left): James Skelton (AB), Thomas McLeod (AB), Petty Officer Arthur Bailey, Petty Officer Robert Forde, and Joseph Leese (AB).

The back row includes (from left): Fireman Angus McDonald, William McDonald (AB), 2nd Engineer William Horton, Stoker William Burton, Stoker Robert Brissenden, Fireman Thomas McGillion, Petty Officer Frederick Parsons, Stoker Edward McKenzie, Petty Officer William Heald, the groom Anton Omelchenko, Steward W. H. Neale, the cook Thomas Clissold, Leading Seaman Albert Balson, Petty Officer John Mather, Mortimer McCarthy (AB), and Leading Shipwright Francis Davies.

Messrs. J. S. Fry & Sons, the famous chocolate manufacturer, was another of the expedition's suppliers. Here (right) in another of Ponting's carefully choreographed shots, three crew members wrapped warmly in matching polar gear are about to enjoy their chocolate allowance. Fry & Sons provided the expedition with "cocoa, sledging and fancy chocolate— delicious comforts, excellently packed and always in good condition." 1910–1912

To get south, Terra Nova (opposite) had to sail through the Roaring Forties, the Furious Fifties, and the Screaming Sixties. Passing through these latitudes could be very uncomfortable for the inexperienced sailor and even for a very experienced seaman. 1912

Cape Crozier (opposite), home to the Emperor penguin colony which so interested Edward Wilson that he, Birdie Bowers, and Apsley Cherry-Garrard made an expedition in mid-winter to it to study the birds' incubation patterns and to gather some of their eggs. The sea and ice conditions at Cape Crozier, located at the eastern end of Ross Island immediately adjacent to the Great Ice Barrier, made it impossible for Scott's party to land there.
JANUARY 3, 1911

Ponting's moving picture film Ninety Degrees South contained footage filmed from the ship (left) of whales that approached Terra Nova, including both killer whales (orcas) and the great Baleen whales that were so attractive to the whaling industry. Whalers had been dipping ever further south in their quest for unexploited populations for some time, although it was only after the 1920s that serious damage was done. Blue whales, in particular, suffered from over-hunting, and many biologists fear the plunder was too great to allow the stocks to recover. Only the very fortunate visitor to the Antarctic will glimpse one of these magnificent animals today, whereas at the time Ponting was filming them, their numbers were estimated to be as high as 240,000.
1910–1912

CHAPTER FOUR

ANTARCTIC PIONEER

H.J.P ("DOUGLAS") ARNOLD

ANTARCTIC PIONEER

H.J.P ("DOUGLAS") ARNOLD

Herbert Ponting in his early 20s, around the time that he unsuccessfully tried to make a living at fruit farming and mining in the United States.

As HERBERT GEORGE PONTING PURSUED HIS CAREER as a talented professional photographer in many lands in the years up to World War I, and capped those experiences in Antarctica during Scott's *Terra Nova* Expedition, it would have been understandable if, during those challenging and sometimes dangerous moments, his mind had not turned briefly to his more comfortable beginnings in the English West Country of the later Victorian years. Indeed, if life had mirrored paternal aspirations, Herbert would have been employed in banking rather than risking life and limb covering wars for the news media or being attacked by killer whales.

His background was certainly not lacking in color—at least on his mother's side. Mary Sydenham came from rich West Country stock, which could boast of Sir Francis Drake in the family line as well as a later physician, Thomas Sydenham, accorded the title of "Father of English Medicine." The Pontings were reputedly of Huguenot extraction and Herbert's grandfather Henry, a former pupil at the prestigious Marlborough School, became an agent to the Marquis of Ailesbury in the Savernake Forest of Wiltshire. Henry's skills were doubtless an example for his eldest son Francis—Herbert's father—who proceeded to make a mark in the world of banking at a time of great expansion. Increasingly senior management posts in various parts of the country charted his success and he was able to leave formal employment in his early fifties and devote himself to furthering his own financial interests. When he died in 1923, aged 81, his estate was worth £45,000—equivalent to some £1.3 million at today's values.

Herbert was born in Salisbury, Wiltshire, on March 21, 1870, the eldest son in a family of four boys and four girls. The family moved around the country from Salisbury to Carlisle as Francis's career developed, and they lived in a manner befitting his status. There were maids, a cook, a gardener, and a coachman, and life was very comfortable. Francis was not interested in political or public life and his work and family were the twin centers of his attention. There were musical evenings, games, and outings for the children, whose parents appear to have been firm but not dominating in the classic Victorian manner. At school none achieved any great distinction and, after leaving college, Herbert entered banking at a local branch in Liverpool. By the end of four years he was convinced that he was not cut out to follow his father's career path, and with Francis's blessing and considerable financial support set out for the west coast of the United States.

No detail has survived about the family discussions that doubtless took place before the decision was taken, or why specifically the United States was chosen. It was significant that Herbert's rejection of banking as a career seems in no way to have alienated his father, and that although some of Herbert's siblings began to be a little irked at living in the shadow of their brother's increasing fame, Francis's pride in his son steadily increased.

When he arrived in California in 1893 or 1894, however, fame and photography still lay some way in the future. Using some of the funds given to him by his father, he purchased a fruit farm, and then invested in a gold mine. A portrait taken at this time shows a rather dashing and suave individual who was doubtless popular with the ladies.

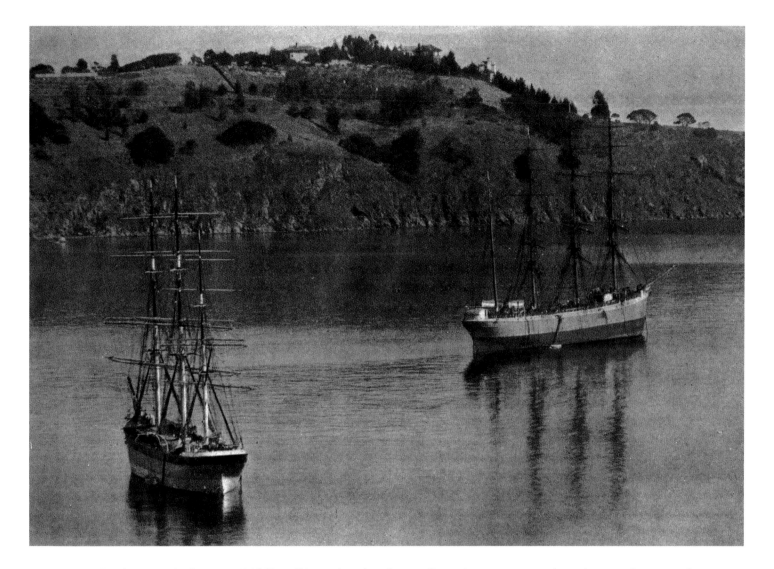

In June 1895, he married Mary Biddle Elliott, the daughter of a US army general, and over the next five years a daughter and a son were born. It was not too long before both the farm and the mine ran into financial difficulties, but by then Herbert had discovered photography.

He took it up seriously in 1900 when, as he wrote in *The Weekly Press* in 1910, "I had to stereograph everything I could. The beautiful stereoscopic process had a hold on me [that] … got stronger and stronger." Ponting applied himself diligently to perfecting his handling of the stereograph technique, in which a specially adapted camera takes two views simultaneously (spaced slightly apart to mimic the separation of the eyes); the resulting pair of photographs is seen through a viewer that combines them into a single, apparently three-dimensional image. Within a short time he was winning prizes for his work—a "telephotograph" of ships in San Francisco Bay shot from his home in Sausalito received recognition from the optical company Bausch & Lomb, while another, a superb shot of "Mules at a Californian Round-up," was featured at a World's Fair by Kodak. A professional photographer advised him to submit examples of his work to specialist steroscope companies. This he did successfully, being "so staggered by the prices offered that I thought this method was the best way of 'scrapping' negatives I had ever known…"

This was the beginning of more than a decade of globe-trotting. In 1901 he went on a tour of the Far East on behalf of the magazine *Leslie's Weekly* and the Universal Photo Art Company of Philadelphia. Not long after his return, Underwood & Underwood, another major publisher of stereo photographs, commissioned him to go to

The ascent of Mount Asama in Japan was one of the most harrowing episodes of Ponting's career. As he and some of the men who had hauled his equipment to the top of the volcano stood near the opening of the crater, a small eruption threw tons of rock upward, accompanied by thick sulphurous fumes. The men with him fled, and Ponting had to follow them to get back his equipment in order to return and record the scene.

Japan, and he took many photographs in Korea and Manchuria too. Then, when the Russo-Japanese War broke out in 1904, he was accredited as a war photographer to the First Japanese Army in Manchuria, working for *Harper's Weekly* and H. C. White & Co. It is impossible to establish the precise chronology of his travels after the Russo-Japanese War ended in 1905, but he was certainly in China and India in 1906–07, and back in Europe, taking mountain photographs in Switzerland and France, in 1908.

Spain, Portugal, Russia, Java, and Burma were other countries to which he was sent on assignment, and the list of magazines and periodicals in which his photographs appeared, both in Britain and the United States, was impressive. It included *Harper's*, *Century*, *World's Work*, *Strand*, *Wide World*, *Metropolitan*, *Cosmopolitan*, *Sunset*, *Pearson's*, *Leslie's Weekly*, *Sphere*, *Illustrated London News*, and *Graphic*. His work was featured in *L'Illustration* and other Continental weeklies, and he was a particularly frequent contributor to *Country Life*.

Often Ponting contributed well-researched articles as well as photographs to the magazines. Where this was not the case, it is now difficult to assess the full body of his work because the captions to the pictures would simply credit the photographic agency, making attribution to a particular photographer difficult. But the power of his work was obvious. The "seeing eye" is a convenient phrase to describe an inherent skill, but Ponting had developed this strongly in his landscape and pictorial work, and his portraits, particularly of craftsmen at work, had considerable impact. Whether tramping up to the top of a mountain over and over again (wielding a heavy camera and large glass-plate negatives) until the conditions were just right, facing acute discomfort, sometimes danger, to get a photograph, or developing negatives to extract the maximum detail and quality from them, he became the complete and dedicated self-taught professional. Ponting had no time for theoretical and often vituperative

No matter where he went, Ponting took a massive armory of equipment to make certain he could take the best photograph possible. Here, he stands atop a 10-foot (3-m) stepladder hauled all the way to the top of a Japanese volcano to obtain just the right angle.

In Japan, Ponting was awed by the mystical power of Mount Fuji. He photographed the volcano from many different angles. When he finally ascended it, he found a view of "indescribable beauty," as the clouds were transfigured into an amazing array of colors and shades as the sun sank through and below them.

arguments about what photography was or was not, or for debates about its status as an art form. Driven at some times by what the market required, and at others by what the imagination directed, Ponting simply sought to always make his images the best. A contemporary distinguished portrait photographer and friend, E. O. Hoppé, perhaps best summed up Ponting's work when he described him as a perfectionist and his own fiercest critic—"the supreme pictorial reporter with a superb technique."

The Russo-Japanese War was undoubtedly the biggest single event in Ponting's career before his involvement in Scott's Antarctic expedition. The limitations of film and cameras of the period mean that the "war" photographs that come down to us cannot compare with the immediacy of those taken today—particularly as on the Japanese side the correspondents and photographers covering the war were not allowed anywhere near the action. However, the war does enable us to see Ponting in action through the eyes of a well-known correspondent colleague, Edwin Emerson, who wrote about Ponting in some detail in his book *Sunset*, published in 1905:

"[He is] the foremost war photographer in the Far East... Ponting is the man, whose exclusive photographs of Port Arthur, Mukden, Manchuria, Korea and the hostile war fleets in eastern waters were published broad-cast [widely] by Underwood and Underwood at the outset of the war. Ponting was the only one who had the gumption to travel through these regions on the eve of the outbreak of hostilities, photographing everything of warlike interest in spite of frequent arrests and danger of prolonged military imprisonment. When war broke out, his unsurpassed stereoscopic pictures of the most important places and men in the theatre of war, were in such demand that the publishers cleared many thousands of dollars, the reproductions appearing in American and European publications....When I first met Ponting in the Far East, he was perched on a high ladder in the midst of a surging mob on the principal square in Tokyo taking photographs of a public reception given by Admiral Togo. Someone nearly upset the ladder. I caught it as it swayed and steadied it. Ponting merely glanced down for an instant and said, 'Thank you, sir'. Later, when I was more formally introduced to him, he told me that he had got so used to being upset with his camera that the danger of such an accident had ceased to have the thrill of novelty."

Photographs of Japanese subjects of a more peaceful kind figured prominently in a number of published collections in the early 1900s; then in 1910, just before setting out for Antarctica, Ponting's book *In Lotus-Land: Japan* was published. In looking at the book it is tempting to see in the superb images of Mount Fuji precursors of what was to follow when he turned his long lenses on Mount Erebus and Mount Lister in the south. Praise for his work was virtually universal but, unbeknown to everybody except his close family, there had already been one casualty of his single-mindedness and dedication to photography—his marriage.

The cover of Ponting's first book, In Lotus-Land: Japan. *The book was published just as Scott's expedition set off for the Antarctic.*

Some time in 1905 or 1906, Ponting returned to the family home in Berkeley, California and told his wife Mary that as an artist, marriage was a millstone around his neck and that he could not be tied down by family responsibilities. He left her, his 9-year-old daughter Mildred, and his son Dick, who was 7, and never returned. After the passage of a century it is impossible to analyze the reasons for the breakdown. There may have been other factors besides his work: Ponting's dedication to causes could become an obsession, but he also seemed incapable of forming deep personal relationships, a lifelong characteristic that was surely fatal to a happy marriage (though he never lacked for female company throughout the ensuing years). His father Francis reacted in a typically forthright manner by supporting Mary and her children financially for the rest of his life, with his son seemingly receiving scant sympathy for his action.

Ponting may well have felt the separation more deeply than first appeared. For example, shortly before going to the Antarctic in 1910, he sent a message to his two children, who were in Europe, that he wished to see them before he left. They came to London but found a note at his hotel saying that he had already left, because, as his son Dick recalled in a letter in 1963, "he felt that if he again saw [them], it might deter his ambition to leave on this hazardous trip." Further regrets were to surface later in his life.

After his return from the 1910–13 expedition, Ponting effectively renounced serious photography—in great contrast to the subsequent activities in both still and motion pictures of Mawson's and Shackleton's photographer, the irrepressible Frank Hurley. This rejection happened despite continuing assignment offers from the likes of *National Geographic* magazine. Why did he act in this way? Was it because, having reached a zenith with his work in the south, he thought that only an artistic decline could lie ahead? It is possible but unlikely. After all, on his return from Antarctica he was still only in his early 40s and reasonably fit. For an inveterate traveler, there was always Everest to contemplate, or the Arctic, or at the opposite climatic extreme, the jungles of Amazonia, given his obvious and new-found talent for recording the world of nature with the motion picture camera.

The main reason for what must have been a conscious decision on his part almost certainly lay back in Antarctica. All the members of the expedition were affected by the deaths of the Polar Party but none, except perhaps Apsley Cherry-Garrard, seem to have been so affected as Herbert Ponting. Ponting was an intensely patriotic individual who passionately valued the virtues that he considered had made the British Empire great—

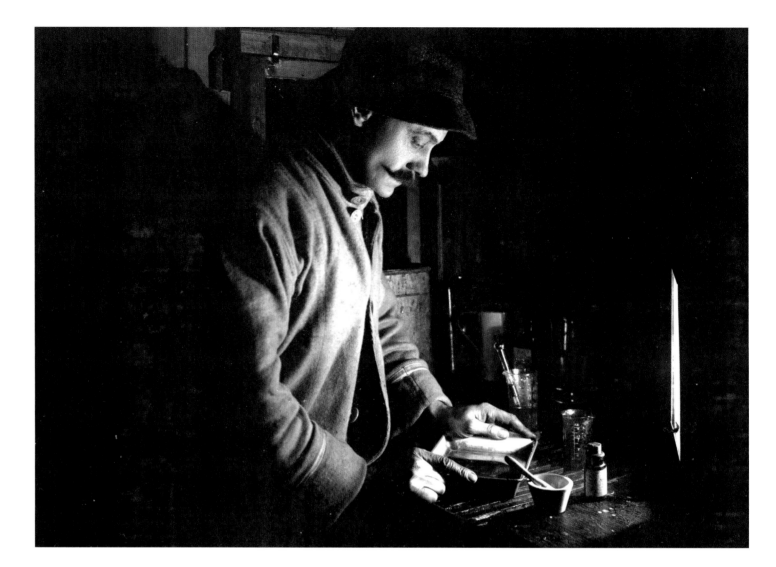

This famous picture of Ponting shows him, as ever, hard at work in his darkroom in the hut at Cape Evans. Ponting's admiration of Scott continued long after his return from the Antarctic, and can be seen in Ponting's preservation of the Polar Party's memory in his photographs in The Great White South, *as well as in his film,* 90° South: With Scott to the Antarctic.

bravery, loyalty, dedication, and a preparedness for self-sacrifice. All of these he saw personified in the five members of the Polar Party who died, and he set out with passion and fervor to try to ensure that remembrance of them would never fade. This he did initially by frequent lectures (complete with film excerpts) and article writing.

Then came the very great success of his illustrated book about Scott's last expedition, *The Great White South,* which, in advance of its publication in 1921, the *British Journal of Photography* promised "would be the most important proof of the immense value of photography in exploration which has hitherto been forthcoming." Having received a copy of the book, the *British Journal of Photography* confirmed it to be "the most eloquent tribute to [Ponting's] artistic and technical skill as a photographer under outdoor conditions such as no other man has been called upon to endure." *The Great White South* had gone through at least 13 editions by 2001.

However, as time went on, Ponting overwhelmingly gave more and more attention to perfecting the motion picture record of the expedition, the rights to which he had purchased from the Gaumont Company in 1914 for £5,000. It was not until as late as 1933, with the release of *90° South: With Scott to the Antarctic,* that the film reached its final version. It is quite clear that in the post-expedition years Antarctica continued to dominate his life to an obsessive extent. The financial aspects of the exploitation of rights from the still pictures of the Scott Expedition are cloaked in confusion (both Ponting and Scott were poor businessmen and no clear written agreement between them was ever concluded), but it seems clear that, overall, Ponting did not make large sums of money out of them.

There is no reason to doubt his claim, for example, that the remake of the film—involving new animation and sound track and adapting the frame rate to a new standard—which took three years to complete and exceeded its budget, cost him £10,000. It was well received by the critics, but was not a commercial success. And, as the events of 1910–13 receded and a new world war began to approach, Ponting's dream became harder and harder to keep alive, particularly when his health began to fail. As he wrote to a friend, "My work for the expedition is now done. I cannot do more. I must try to do something to retrieve the years I have devoted to it. But it is not easy, at my age. It has left me just about ruined."

But the fact that Ponting effectively renounced traveling the world with his camera and looked ever backward to Antarctica does not mean that he did not attempt new ventures—though it might have been better if he had not. One failed business venture followed another, as Ponting heard about new inventions, invested in them, and promoted them with characteristic gusto, if questionable judgment. When in 1926 Ponting wrote to expedition member Frank Debenham that "my only pleasure and joy is in creating things, not selling them" he should perhaps have appreciated the wisdom of his own words.

THE "PONCO"
Unburstable Inner Tube
PATENTED

The Greatest Advance in
Motor Traction since the
Invention of the Pneumatic Tyre

THE
"PONCO" INNER TUBE
Overcomes every trouble to which the
Pneumatic Tyre has hitherto been sub=
ject. When its use becomes general its
Burst=proof and Skid=proof qualities
will save thousands of lives yearly

SAFETY FIRST !

Thus, from the early 1920s to the early 1930s there was a mushroom farm that failed; the Kinatome—an innovative cartridge-film-loading movie projector that failed primarily because it needed a non-standard film gauge; the Variable Controllable Distortagraph—an optical device for creating distortions and caricatures of faces and figures via both movie cameras and projectors, which Ponting thought were hilarious, but which did not impress the industry; and the "Ponco" Inner Tube—an allegedly unburstable tire that got as far as trials with London Transport before its failings became clear.

Such failures would perhaps have depressed even a convinced optimist, but life for Ponting, comfortably located in a bachelor flat close to Oxford Circus in London's West End, was not without its enjoyable times. As in the past, he never formed close relationships, but he had a circle of friends—most with a scholarly or general interest in exploration and Antarctica (such as the Revd. George Seaver, later the biographer of three members of the Polar Party)—in whose company he could relax or dine and discuss the latest news. More interesting perhaps was the relationship he formed with George Ford, the engineer he employed on various projects. Ponting liked to visit Ford and his family bearing small gifts, and appeared to relish spending a few hours in a family setting of warmth and love, which as a father he had never enjoyed himself. It was George's wife Jeanne Ford who, on seeing Ponting's reaction to a distortion produced by the prototype Distortagraph, commented revealingly: "I didn't think he could laugh!" Yet he was remembered fondly by colleagues and employees. C. H. Dickason, his last photographic assistant (Ponting still occasionally took portraits of friends) recalled in 1964 that: "As a chief he was wonderful to work with

Ponting patented a device that he called the Variable Controllable Distortagraph. This image of Charlie Chaplin (above) shows how it could caricature famous personalities. Like so many of his inventions, it fell flat.

and almost anybody could approach him. He was a perfect gentleman and his breeding was evident always… [I was] thrilled and proud of the opportunity to work for a man whose work in the field of pictorial photography was without a shadow of doubt second to none."

As the 1930s progressed Ponting's health began to fail. He may well have developed diabetes, and he eventually died of heart failure on February 7, 1935. Just a few weeks before his death he wrote to Frank Debenham at the Scott Polar Research Institute in Cambridge "…I want to arrange that in the event of my death at any time, the ownership of all my Antarctic negatives shall rest in the Polar Institute … I must get my solicitor to make out a legal document embodying this." He did not do so and after his death the material was eventually purchased by a photo agency. He left a number of legacies (including bequests to his son and daughter) that totaled several thousand pounds, but the net value of his estate before the sale of photographic equipment and pictures was only a little over £377—the small sum seeming to symbolize the disparity between Ponting's abilities and his accomplishments. His was a life that achieved much, but which surely could have achieved even more.

Ponting, the "Camera Artist"

When in 1909 Robert Scott was evaluating potential members of his second expedition to Antarctica, Herbert Ponting's name was almost certainly known to him by reputation. A much published photographer, Ponting would write subsequently in *The Great White South* (1921) with typical immodest modesty, "my life [before going to Antarctica]—save for six years' ranching and mining in western America; a couple of voyages round the world; three years of travel in Japan; some months as war correspondent with the First Japanese Army during the war with Russia; and in the Philippines during the American war with Spain; and save, too, for several years of travel in a score of other lands—had been comparatively uneventful." The immediate link with Scott, however, doubtless stemmed from Cecil Meares, an equally experienced traveler who had been placed in charge of the expedition's

The progress Terra Nova *made through the ice pack was so slow that Ponting was able to leave the ship and take photos of her. Here Ponting was photographed in action.*

dogs, and who had journeyed with Ponting in Asia some years before. When at their first meeting in the fall of 1909 Scott told Ponting that he considered photography to be of such importance that it was his intention to make a special department of the art—and invited him to take charge of it—there could have been no doubt about the response, even though a lucrative trip around the Empire for a newspaper group was in the offing. As Ponting wrote in *The Great White South*, "…I felt that this was a chance, such as never would come to me again, to turn the experience that I had gained to some permanent benefit to science, and that I was convinced that if I went, and were given a free hand to utilise my experience as I thought best, the photographic results might prove to be not only of great educational value, but a valuable [financial] asset to the enterprise."

Ponting spent the first half of 1910 gathering together a comprehensive selection of movie and still cameras, together with accessories and film, such that he could meet every scientific and general situation he was likely to encounter. One newspaper, the *West Australian*, described it as "the most perfect photographic equipment ever devised" while the *British Journal of Photography,* a little more circumspectly, referred in its June 1910 issue to an outfit "the like of which has probably never before been brought together." Teddy Evans, second-in-command to Scott, put it more boldly—"A colossal photographic outfit." The young geologist Frank Debenham, who in due course was to take over many of Ponting's photographic responsibilities during the Expedition's second year, and later still to head the Scott Polar Research Institute, early in the trip wrote perhaps a little enviously in his diary, published as *The Quiet Land: The Antarctic Diaries of Frank Debenham*: "[Ponting's] photos will be quite the most popular part of the Expedition for he has some perfectly marvellous instruments... One camera has a set of about 10 lenses and, as it has a large extension, he can do anything with it, from photomicrography [to] stereoscopic work."

A lengthy stay in Antarctica, particularly before the era of wireless communication, was a challenging experience involving a sense of separation perhaps comparable to a lengthy mission aboard a submarine or spacecraft. Ponting's character had both negative and positive elements in facing such a trial. Unlike the gregarious Frank Hurley, he was basically a "loner" with a stiff and slightly fussy demeanor and without a marked sense of humor. Again unlike Hurley, he could never be regarded as a "team player"—and it is significant that he never attended any of the reunions held from 1925 onward by the survivors of the Scott Expedition. His background provided him with the manners that enabled him to fit easily into social gatherings, but for the most part he preferred to relentlessly pusue his chosen path without distractions from persons or events. He was set in his ways, so in the confined spaces both on the ship and in the hut much friction was created with his colleagues.

However, even if he was irked by the lack of physical activity during an Antarctic winter, dedication to his work provided some outlet. He built his own darkroom in the hut at Cape Evans and it became his personal area with a camp-bed for sleeping at night. This was done with the blessing of Scott, who wrote in his diary on April 13, 1911: "Such a palatial chamber [it was all of 8 feet long, 6 feet wide, and 8 feet high, or 2.4 by 1.8 by 2.4 m] for the development of negatives and prints can only be justified by the quality of the work produced in it, and is only justified in our case by the possession of such an artist as Ponting...." Scott commented on the neatness of everything, to which Ponting responded with typical candor: "...in matters photographic untidiness is abhorrent to me." It was there that he worked, and the processing of movie film in particular, while in some ways tedious, became a welcome way of consuming time during the long dark hours.

In the 1920s, Newman-Sinclair advertised their cine cameras by using a film strip of Ponting's footage from the Antarctic. Although the camera shown in the advertisement (above) was not identical to the cinematograph that Ponting took south with him, it would not have been dissimilar.

In the hut at Cape Evans, Ponting built an 8 x 6-foot (2.4 x 1.8-m) room (left) that served as the photographic darkroom and storage facility, as well as his sleeping area. The room was packed with equipment, clear up to its ceiling.

Ponting started his careful documentation of the expedition immediately upon joining the ship. Even during the gale on the voyage south, when there were fears that Terra Nova *would* founder, he was hard at work.

Ponting's encounter with killer whales gave him some of the most terrifying moments of his life. He had to leap from floe to floe toward the ship, with the whales snorting and blowing only a few yards behind him. His escape to safety was immortalized in this painting (left) by Ernest Linzeli.

Ponting's single-mindedness could have led to strained relations with other expedition members and the fact that it mostly did not speaks volumes for both sides. There was potential for problems at the very outset of the arrival in Antarctica, when Scott told Ponting to take advantage of the good weather to pursue his photographic activities rather than taking any part in the unloading of the ship. This inevitably caused some mutterings among the other members, which would probably not have occurred if the leader had communicated his decision more widely. There was in any case a quid pro quo. Ponting had to move all of his equipment and supplies ashore unaided as well as conduct his immediate photographic program—and it is noticeable that quite frequently thereafter he proceeded unaccompanied on various photographic trips, dragging the heavy photo sled without help.

Ponting gained respect for his determination to get pictures, even in circumstances of considerable danger. Aboard *Terra Nova*, expedition members watched fascinated as a platform was rigged up off the bow so that he could use the cinematograph to film the ship smashing through the ice floes. There is an image of the vessel shot during the storm that enveloped them shortly after leaving New Zealand, securing which must have exposed Ponting to considerable danger. (This same storm saw him trying to safeguard his valuable equipment and supplies while most other crew members were working pumps to save the ship—a poor sailor, he was described by Scott as "developing plates with the developing dish in one hand and an ordinary [sick] basin in the other!"). In due course, a dangerous close encounter with killer whales, and an occasion when he secured a picture despite the danger from the breakup of ice underfoot, became generally known among the small community and increased their regard for Ponting. The overwhelming impression is that most regarded him as a little odd, but also with some affection. Thus

Ponting never forgot his flight from the killer whales. Years later, he replayed for the camera his exact movements while posing under much less dangerous circumstances (above).

Ponting was dubbed "Jonah" because of the accidents that seemed to befall expedition members when posing for his cameras and, as noted in chapter 2, the geologist Griffith Taylor invented a new verb for the process of being an uncomfortable subject of the photographer's camera: "to pont." Ponting's popularity grew with each of his lectures on exotic foreign lands, and Cecil Meares composed a poem about him (reproduced in 1969 in *Photographer of the World*, by H. J. P. Arnold). The first verse and chorus reflect the affection in which Ponting came to be held:

> *I'll sing a little song, about one among our throng,*
> *Whose skill in making pictures is not wanting.*
> *He takes pictures while you wait, "prices strictly moderate;"*
> *I refer, of course, to our Professor Ponting.*

> *Then pont, Ponko, pont and long may Ponko pont;*
> *With his finger on the trigger of his "gadget."*
> *For whenever he's around, we're sure to hear the sound*
> *Of his high-speed cinematographic ratchet.*

For all his single-mindedness, Ponting was more than capable of accepting the fun being poked at him, and could reciprocate in kind, commenting in *The Great White South* that, "The saving grace of humour served us in good stead always." And it is noticeable that, while privately in later years he criticized Scott for poor financial management of the expedition, and publicly in a restrained way entered the argument about the under-use of dogs, Ponting did not utter a word of criticism about any of his colleagues in *The Great White South*. Indeed, he went out of his way to pay tribute to their sterling character and skills.

Ponting regarded instructing his colleagues in the mechanics of photography to be an essential part of his duties. Like most professionals, he would doubtless not have taken too kindly to being interrupted when working, but at other times he gave generously of his time and expertise. Scott wrote at some length in his diary about Ponting's photography lessons: "My incursion into photography has brought me in close contact with [Ponting] and I realise what a very good fellow he is; no pains are too great for him to take to help and instruct others, whilst his enthusiasm for his own work is unlimited… The photography craze is in full swing. Ponting's mastery is ever more impressive, and his pupils improve day by day; nearly all of us have produced good negatives. Debenham and Wright are the most promising but Taylor, Bowers and I are also getting the hang of the tricky exposures." (It was Scott and Bowers who exposed the last photographs of the Polar Party on its journey, Ponting having instructed them on "how to release the shutter by means of a long thread so that all … might appear in the group…")

Since Ponting was scheduled to leave as planned with several other members of the expedition when *Terra Nova* returned early in 1912 (the ship setting out for New Zealand again in mid-March), there was a need to train his replacements. All of his "pupils" were encouraged, but Frank Debenham was the star. He showed, wrote Ponting in *The Great White South*, a "capacity for taking pains that was soon productive of the most encouraging results … aided by a genuine affection for photography, and the recognition that it could be of much value to him in his science—(he) rapidly absorbed all that I was able to impart as to the primary principles, and ere summer came he … produced beautiful photographs of really difficult subjects." This was soundly based and generous encouragement from a master—to whose own "beautiful photographs" we now turn.

Ponting came to Antarctica with a fund of proven and valuable experience—and the essential prerequisites of determination and infinite patience. The first professional or specialist photographer to visit the continent, he had been provided with the best equipment and film available in his day. It is natural to assume that the equipment he used could not possibly compare with that of the present day. This is not entirely accurate; while unwieldy and heavy, the cameras and lenses were capable of producing high-quality results. A far more critical factor was to be found in the glass-plate and celluloid film stock. The science of sensitometry was still evolving and a concentrated study of plate and film characteristics was only just beginning. Thus, much photography was still conducted using orthochromatic material, which was highly sensitive to the blue end of the visible spectrum and thus, for example, often led to totally overexposed skies if used without filters. Panchromatic material, which also recorded longer wavelengths toward the red end of the spectrum, was becoming available but the carefully designed, balanced reproduction which can now routinely be achieved did not then exist—which placed a high premium on experience. Ponting had this in plenty.

Ponting used a telephoto lens to get this shot of Mount Lister and the lesser peaks in front of it from 70 miles (130 km) away at McMurdo Sound. He also caught a grounded iceberg in the foreground.

Ponting did not write in his books or articles about his philosophy of photography—if, indeed, he had such a thing—but it is possible from his pictures to deduce something of his thought processes and actions. In his landscape photography—which is undoubtedly his supreme achievement—he did not look *at* a scene so much as *into* it. He obviously assessed the different colors and how they would reproduce in black and white; studied the planes of perspective; and analyzed whether benefit would be derived from a different vantage point, at the same time calculating what should be included in the frame: would the end result benefit, for example, from a foreground "lead in?" In short, he must have been visualizing the result in black and white in much the same way as, some decades later, Ansel Adams was doing in the wilderness regions of another continent.

To take just one example, we can follow this thought process in action—together with reference to the difficulties and frustrations encountered—through his own words in *The Great White South*:

"Scott told me that a panoramic telephotograph of the [mountain] range would be of lasting value to geography. I knew it would also be a remarkable feat of photography. I had soon realised the difficult nature of the task, however, for in those first sunny summer days the radiation from the sea had been so great that the quivering air rendered telephotography of distant objects impossible. One day in the autumn I had succeeded, however, in telephotographing … Mt. Lister, over 13,000 feet high and seventy miles away, during a brief lull in the wind. But, for the coveted panorama [of the range] I had to wait until the weather became colder; and when it did so, the few days on which the mountains appeared clearly were so windy that the feat was equally impracticable.… An equivalent focus of nearly six feet would have to be used—six magnifications of an eleven-inch lens, which took the extreme limit of the extension of my camera. A six-times colour filter would be necessary in conjunction with an orthochromatic plate, and a medium diaphragm. Photographic enthusiasts will understand that to attempt to use such a combination on a windy day would be to court certain failure. Moreover, it was necessary that the picture should be taken from as great height as possible; for the tendency of telephotography is to annihilate perspective, and from sea-level the intervening icebergs would appear to be close to the mountains, some of which were about ninety miles away. I should therefore have to get above the highest of them [the icebergs]. This increased the difficulty, for the wind was invariably stronger on high ground. I selected a position on the Erebus moraine, above the Ramp, where, in the lee of a debris-cone, there would be, to some extent, shelter from the prevailing wind, if any, and an uninterrupted prospect from an altitude of about 250 feet.

"To accomplish the feat had become for the time being the principal aim of my existence, and I had kept a watchful eye on the weather, in the hope that, if but for one single hour, the elements might prove propitious. But, to my disappointment, the winter had crept upon us without any chance having occurred to attain the object of my desire. [With the return of the Sun] … the yearning to record the wonder was greater than ever; but week after week passed by, and still no opportunity occurred. On the rare occasions when the wind was at rest and the mountains visible, the radiation from the ice was now as bad as formerly it had been from the open water. It was impossible to focus. As it was now mid-summer again, I began to fear I might never get the coveted picture; for, once the ice broke up, the character of the scene would be completely changed. A frozen sea was essential.

"But early in January there came a day when the visibility was perfect, and only a light breeze, sufficient to eliminate all radiation, was blowing. I decided that the chance of a lifetime had come; so 'packing' my things up to the Ramp, I set the camera on a heavy, rigid tripod in the shelter of my debris cone. All the peaks stood out distinctly in the marvellously clear air; but the sea edge of the glaciers—at the base of the foothills, 40 miles across the Sound—was invisible … below the horizon.

"After carefully checking some calculations, I exposed a double series of 7 x 5

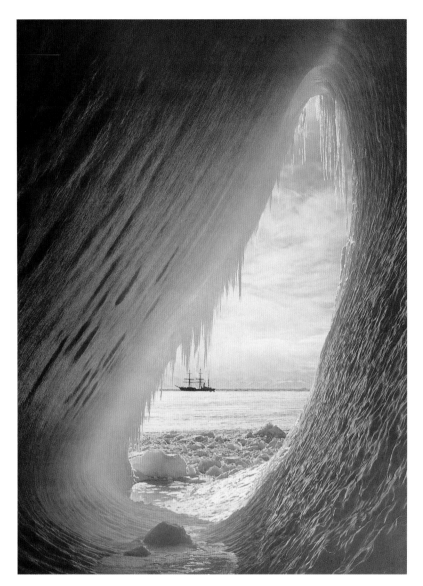

Few pictures of the Antarctic are more memorable than those Ponting took from inside an ice grotto near Cape Evans. In this carbon print, the pastel green tones of the ice grotto set off the Terra Nova, *which appears in the distance, perfectly composed below the dripping icicles.*

plates on the panorama, telephotographing the entire range from end to end; and I had the satisfaction of developing, an hour later, twelve beautiful negatives of one of the longest-distance panoramic telephotographs ever secured." An example of these telephotographs is reproduced on the previous page and on pages 126–127.

Ponting's application and patience were always of a high order and, when contemplating the ease with which photographs can be taken today, this description tempts one to make the perhaps unfair generalization that the quality of a result is often in inverse ratio to the ease with which it was obtained.

While the reproductions published widely over the years have often not done the originals justice, Ponting's meticulous approach achieved much success across most of his pictorial and landscape images. He had his favorites (he deemed there to be "none more beautiful" than the series of the ice "grotto") but we only have to look at a few of the classics—such as "Midnight Sun in the Ross Sea," "Death of an Iceberg," "Freezing of the Sea," and "Christmas Eve in the Pack"—to see how consummately he handled difficult subjects. There is scarcely a single

Ponting landscape which has an empty sky; if the Sun is included in the frame the bleed or glare effect is limited; and despite extreme contrast in a scene, usually there will be detail in both highlights and shadows. Ponting's claim to being called a "camera artist," rather than a photographer, may seem pretentious but it was justified by his results—which were matchless when printed in pastel tones of blue or green by the carbon process.

Edward Wilson, chief of the expedition's science staff, was a talented artist but even he found benefit in Ponting's skills: "I remember how puzzled [Wilson] once was over one of his studies of Mt. Erebus," Ponting wrote. "He could not get the mountain to look high enough. My experience in photographing mountains showed me what was wrong. He had given the sketch too much sky. Taking a sheet of paper I placed it across the top of his drawing, cutting off three inches, and immediately the mountain rose. He was quite pleased, and thought it remarkable that he had not thought of such a simple expedient himself."

Ponting belonged to a school of photography which in many ways was not regarded as "artistic" by the aesthetic conventions of the time: he did not indulge in tricks or composites and sought straight, crisp effects with maximum depth of field and technically rigorous development. Yet in later years an art journal could write that "Mr Ponting's pictures possess qualities which are only looked for in the work of great painters" and a noted member of the Royal Academy, Sir John Lavery, after looking at a Ponting portfolio, was quoted as saying that, "If I were to have painted any of these scenes, I would not have altered either the composition or the lighting of any of them in any way whatsoever." This was testimony to Ponting's superlative ability to visualize, record, and reproduce a scene on paper with incomparable technical excellence.

While landscape photography revealed Ponting as a complete master, other areas of his work were also of a high order. Hitherto his work as a portraitist has not been emphasized, but in fact some of his studies were superb: we see Meares showing the strain of exposure to the Antarctic elements, but looking with clear eyes and the gaze of an experienced, hardy traveler; there is Cherry-Garrard, returned from a challenging journey who looks at Ponting's camera with the somewhat less assured, although bright expression of a younger man; and there are several portraits of "Soldier" Oates, which somehow manage to reveal his complex character—resolute and to a degree inscrutable, but with a sardonic comment about to be brought forth. Images of everyday activities are less likely to aspire to the categories of high art, but they appear in the collection in great numbers—ranging from a festive dinner scene to excruciatingly cold outside work in the height of winter, and all characterized by clarity and maximum detail. "Atmosphere" is difficult to define but it is also there in many of the pictures—most impressively of all perhaps in the image of Oates and Meares contentedly smoking their pipes as they converse at the blubber stove, where we can almost feel the welcome warmth and smell the pungent aroma!

In his movie work—and in particular that devoted to portraying the fauna of Antarctica—Ponting revealed the same qualities inherent in his still work. A novice in motion pictures before Antarctica, he made sure that he

Cecil Meares (above), photographed on his return with the support party for Scott's Southern Journey. Meares was in charge of the dogs until he left the expedition in 1912, at the same time as Ponting.

received expert tuition before his departure and obviously practiced the techniques of the moving picture extensively before leaving. Much of his movie record was devoted to seals, penguins, and flying birds, and he demonstrated endless patience and persistence in achieving results that portrayed the life and death of the animals with a detail never before seen. As with still photography, the cinematographer's life was not always without incident, with attacks threatened from seals, skuas, and killer whales, thankfully without serious consequences.

It is natural to attempt a comparison between Ponting and Frank Hurley, as near contemporaries in the Antarctic. It needs to be emphasized that Ponting had significant advantages. He was far more experienced than Hurley—which was of great importance in dealing with the photographic procedures of the time—but even more important was the fact that while Ponting was allowed to do his photographic work to the exclusion of everything else, Hurley was a full member of Shackleton's 1914–17 *Endurance* expedition with activities thrust upon him that had nothing to do with photography. Thus Hurley was not infrequently forced to "snatch" pictures when he could, whereas Ponting could take time to strive for the perfect result. Moreover, the circumstances in which Hurley found himself as the *Endurance* saga unfolded were infinitely more stressful and demanding than anything Ponting faced—and extended further than being forced to destroy many hard-won plates. The record that Hurley made of the Shackleton expedition was a supreme achievement in the face of extremely adverse conditions. Moreover, as a member of that expedition from start to finish, Hurley's record is more complete than Ponting's, with images shot of events on Elephant Island, for example, having enormous impact.

Where Ponting's work is undoubtedly superior is where he was able to maximize the advantage of time—with the carefully visualized landscapes of high technical quality. While Ponting's skies are rarely empty, many of Hurley's are—showing almost certainly that he was not using one of the yellow or orange "screens" (filters) whose purpose was to darken the sky and render details of cloud. Ponting generally had a surer touch with composition and there is a suggestion in the extreme contrast of many of Hurley's pictures that Ponting was also more careful in processing film and plates—although once again this may partially result from the conditions under which Hurley was forced to work. Perhaps it would be appropriate to compare the relative merits of the two men (who subsequently evinced a high regard for each other's work) by a reference to mathematics: Ponting strove to get every picture 95 percent right as an absolute minimum, whatever the circumstances, while Hurley was content with 80 percent because it afforded more flexibility and speed. There is much to be said for both attitudes.

The comparison between the two contemporaries can be extended to place their—and particularly Ponting's—work in the context of photography in the Antarctic over the following century. There are now many research stations on the continent, and while by no means without danger, life there is infinitely more congenial for the scientists and others visiting and wintering there than for the early explorers. Photography—whether moving or still pictures—is virtually without exception in color.

So far as motion pictures are concerned, Ponting and Hurley must be regarded as trail blazers who were using equipment and film that have long been superseded by many systems up to our own time—where even now video is increasingly replacing film itself. But the situation as regards color still photography is by no means so clear cut. Color film (and digital camera color) is now of extremely high quality. While expeditions to Antarctica have long since declined in numbers, being replaced by long-term residencies at research stations, there are now many temporary residents taking color images for professional, technical, and personal reasons—and visits by professional photographers to take pictures for commercial photo libraries are by no means uncommon. Do their efforts supersede the black and white work of Herbert Ponting?

Paradoxically, the question is best answered in the work of a later professional photographer, the Swiss Emil Schulthess. He visited Antarctica during the International Geophysical Year (1957–58) and was accredited to the US Deep Freeze IV operation. A few years later he published an excellent collection of images in his *Antarctica: A Photographic Survey*. Schulthess shot both in black and white and in color. Much of the color work is as good as one would expect, with carefully chosen bright, colored clothing, and painted objects—such as tractors or helicopters—aiding the impact. But it is the black and white landscapes of icebergs and ice formations generally that impress infinitely more, and the quality of Schulthess's black and white work comes very close to rivaling that of Ponting. In the book, spreads of color are next to spreads of black and white and without exception the texture and tone of the latter are superior. Since the same skill was at work with both mediums, why was this? Almost certainly because, much of the time, Antarctica in broad daylight can be compared to the moon—it is an essentially monochromatic subject. In good conditions, the blue sky reflects off ice and water and the result often is an essay in a narrow range of blue tones, which can be rendered just as well in black and white and frequently with more impact.

Ponting and Hurley both took samples of one of the first practical color systems—Autochrome plates—to the Antarctic with them. The plates had a relatively short life, and color fidelity and quality were such that the plates could best be regarded as showing a promise for the future. But images which both photographers exposed of evening skies pointed to the one area where color photography in the Antarctic comes into its own. Ponting expressed disappointment at what he saw as his failure to obtain pictures of the aurora during the winter.

Over forty years later George Lowe, photographer on the British Trans-Antarctic Expedition, described in his book *Because It Is There* (published in 1959) the fall as "the answer to a colour photographer's prayer, with orange

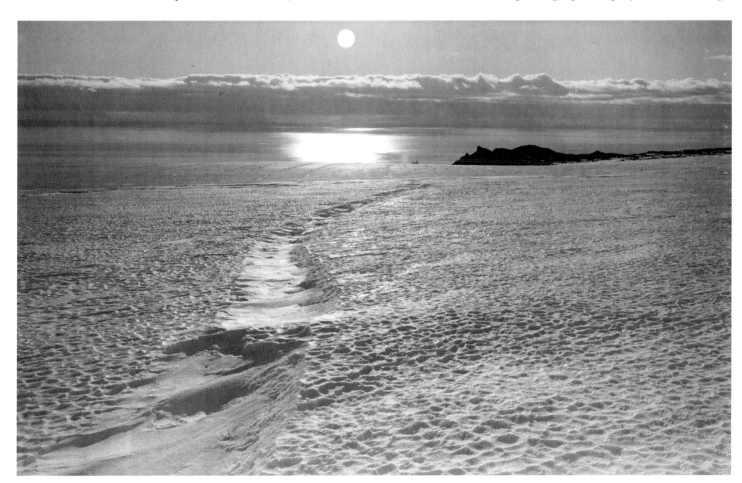

This haunting photograph was taken from, rather than of, one of Ponting's favorite subjects, the Barne Glacier. In the distance toward the northwest, dark against the sunlight, lies Cape Barne.

Ponting was perhaps the first photographer truly to do justice to the natural wonders of the Antarctic, whether on land, or in the sea or—in this case—in the heavens. Although he was disappointed in general with his images of the aurora, one finds it difficult to believe that anyone would not be pleased with this particular photograph.

suns jerking and sizzling through strange mirages, golden snow beneath clouds of every conceivable colour—and the moon always in view, switching on like a lighthouse when dusk fell."

Atmospheric phenomena and their effect upon Earth are indeed a subject for the color camera. Ponting would have relished the use of present-day color film in Antarctica, but he would have used it where it was best suited. Almost certainly he would still find a major role for black and white photography; it is often regarded as the true art medium for photography, a view reinforced by its continued use by photographers today.

As soon as Ponting's still and motion-picture work was publicly presented, the response, from King George V downward, was uniformly favorable, as it had been in Antarctica when he showed expedition members some of the early processed images. Perhaps the most apt response was that of Frank Hurley himself, who arrived in London in November 1916 on his safe return from the *Endurance* expedition. He attended Ponting's lecture-film *With Captain Scott in the Antarctic* four times and wrote in his diary that the pictures "were the acme of photographic perfection... The show well deserves its world-wide merit, Ponting's manner and delivery being excellent." The two met and the Englishman gave the Australian a copy of *In Lotus-Land: Japan* inscribed—with a glance back to his years in the American West—"In tribute to a brother artist of the trail." Hurley was delighted by this and, despite his own undoubted achievements, recorded in *Once More Upon My Adventure* (published in 1966) that "Ponting was looked upon as being the leader in Antarctic photography." (Ponting repaid the compliment years later in 1930 when he wrote to a friend that "Hurley is a 'crackerjack' with the camera.")

222

Ponting himself expressed some regrets about his achievement. "I found the Antarctic a very disappointing region for photography," he wrote in *The Great White South*. "It was exasperating to find the weather so often thwart one when half-way to some goal—for a journey to a point even a few miles distant could not be undertaken lightly. My camera and kinematograph equipment weighed more than 200 lbs: and when visiting a point a few miles away it was wise to take camping kit and food for several days, lest a blizzard should descend upon us. Pulling a load of 400 lbs deadweight, two men could not maintain a greater pace than one mile per hour; and if the surface were bad their progress might be much slower … there was seldom a man available to help me with the photographic work, whereas in fine weather I could have used the services of two constantly. However, notwithstanding the many impediments with which Nature sought to baulk one, it was surprising how much could be accomplished by persistent effort, and by grasping every opportunity she gave whilst in more amicable humour."

Of course he accomplished much, but from a distance of almost a century it is possible to wish—such was the quality of his work—that he could have achieved even more. The drive for perfection had its drawbacks, and in explaining why he abandoned a plan to go with one of the sledging parties he wrote in *The Great White South* "The … journey would not have enabled me to take my own time over my work and photography in these regions is too important and difficult to be done in haste." Perhaps, but the historical record is the poorer for the fact that, despite the valiant efforts of such as Frank Debenham and Murray Levick, there was no Ponting to record the achievement and suffering of the various sledging parties—or to record for posterity, with his typical striking clarity, the faces of the Northern Party when they staggered toward the hut at Cape Evans in November 1912 after surviving an Antarctic winter in appalling circumstances—an achievement that went almost unnoticed in the tragic events that overwhelmed the expedition. If Ponting had gone with the southern parties the record might have been enriched by images of the five members of the Polar Party as they set out on their final journey—but of course Scott did not announce his choice for that party until the last moment, and even if Ponting had begun the journey it is most unlikely that, doubtless refusing to jettison most of his equipment, he would have managed to get that far. What must be readily acknowledged is that Hurley's record of the *Endurance* expedition is more complete (despite the enforced destruction of the negatives they could not carry with them) because of his presence throughout, save for the perilous trip to South Georgia.

A visual record is inevitably seen subsequently in the context of what it portrays, a factor that can powerfully enhance the impact of that record. Thus Hurley's achievement in Antarctica, quite apart from considerations of intrinsic merit, is seen against the backdrop of an expedition that can be fairly described as a brilliant failure—Shackleton got his companions home even if the expedition objectives were not fulfilled and *Endurance* did not survive. If the analogy is brought somewhat closer to the present on another frontier of exploration, we see Hurley's images in the same context as we look at images of the Apollo 13 mission to the Moon.

Ponting's images are on another plane—on that same one from which we look at pictures of the Apollo 1 fire at Cape Kennedy in 1967 or those of the Challenger and Columbia space shuttle disasters of 1986 and 2003. Whatever such images may actually show, we cannot separate them in our minds from our awareness of the tragic loss of life that took place off-camera.

That is why it is appropriate to end with the often-quoted words that Apsley Cherry-Garrard so elegantly and poignantly penned for his obituary of Ponting in the *Geographical Journal* in 1935:

"He came to do a job, did it and did it well. Here in these pictures is beauty linked to tragedy—one of the great tragedies—and the beauty is inconceivable for it is endless and runs to eternity."

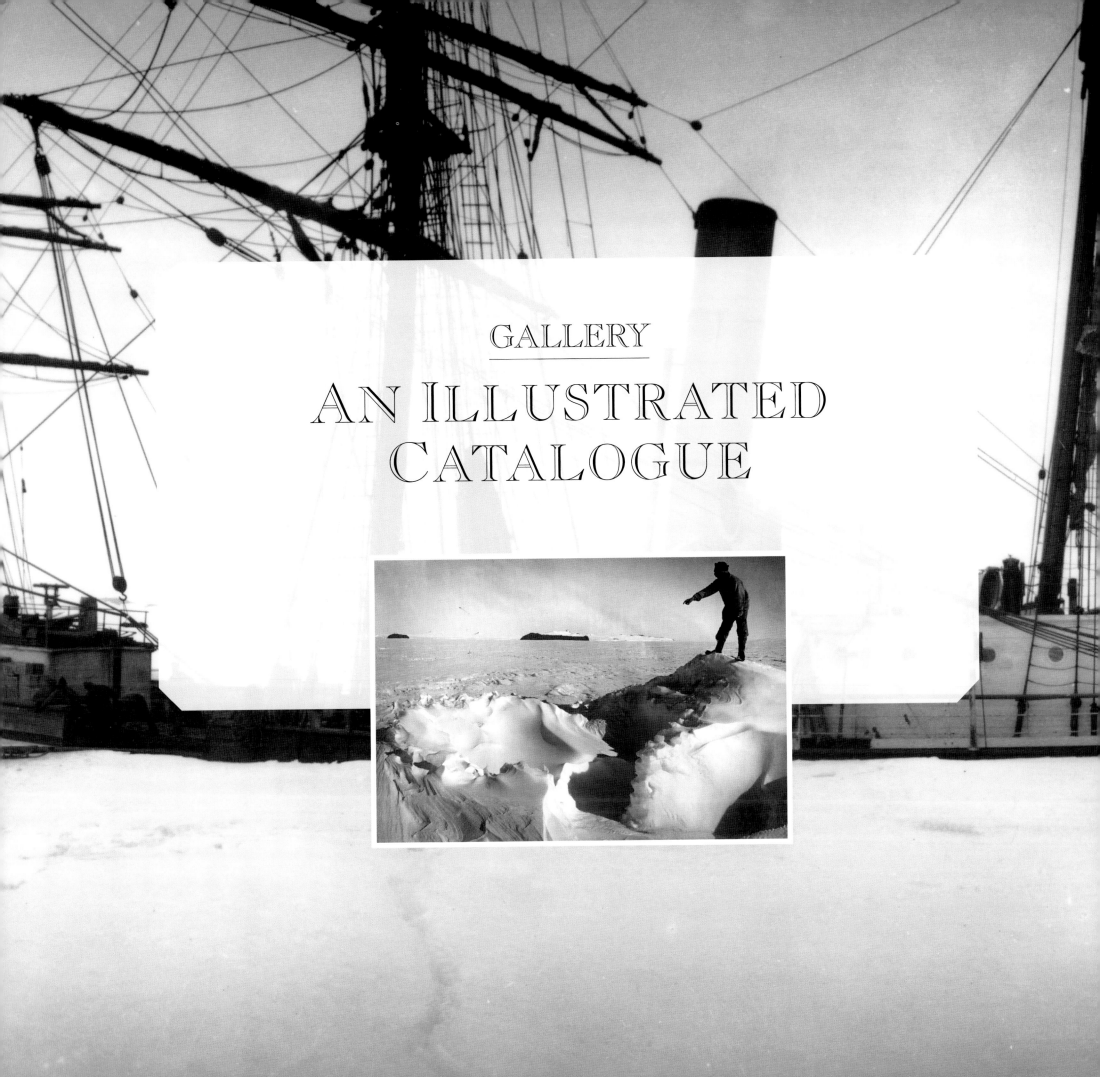

GALLERY

AN ILLUSTRATED
CATALOGUE

GALLERY

THE PHOTOGRAPHS TAKEN BY HERBERT PONTING ON SCOTT'S *TERRA NOVA* EXPEDITION, 1910–1913 IN THIS BOOK ARE DRAWN MOSTLY FROM THE ARCHIVES OF THE ROYAL GEOGRAPHICAL SOCIETY AND THE SCOTT POLAR RESEARCH INSTITUTE. THE FOLLOWING PAGES SHOW PHOTOGRAPHS FROM THE ROYAL GEOGRAPHICAL SOCIETY'S COLLECTION THAT ARE NOT SHOWN ELSEWHERE IN THE BOOK. AFTER EACH CAPTION THERE IS AN ARCHIVE NUMBER FOR REFERENCE.

The *Terra Nova*

Terra Nova sailing through the pack, December 11, 1910. *[A108/000751; SP4059]*

Terra Nova held up in the pack, December 13, 1910. *[A108/000763; SP4071]*

Furling *Terra Nova's* upper topsail in the pack, December 1910. *[A108/001303; SP4611]*

Doctor Wilson and Lieutenant Pennell salting seal skins, December 27, 1910. *[A108/000775; SP4083]*

Lieutenant Rennick and the sounding machine, December 1910. *[A108/001291; SP4599]*

Terra Nova held up for the first time in the ice, December 11, 1910. *[A108/000753; SP4061]*

Terra Nova at ice foot. Cape Barne and glacier in background, January 15, 1911. *[A108/000868; SP4176]*

Watering *Terra Nova* at Glacier Tongue, January 1911. *[A108/001318; SP4626]*

Lillie at the water bottle winch, January 1, 1911. *[A108/000794; SP4102]*

Terra Nova held up in the pack. Ice point in the foreground, December 13, 1910. *[A108/000761; SP4069]*

Terra Nova at ice foot off Hut Point, 1912. *[A108/001275; SP4583]*

Terra Nova at ice foot (fine clouds) and Cape Barne, January 15, 1911. *[A108/001520; SP4828]*

Nelson putting out the water bottle, January 1, 1911. *[A108/000795; SP4103]*

A fish is seen from the deck of *Terra Nova*, December 1910. *[A108/001295; SP4603]*

Bosun Cheetham and ice anchor, December 1910. *[A108/001298; SP4606]*

Mutton hanging in the shrouds on the deck of *Terra Nova*, December 1910. *[A108/001299; SP4607]*

Group on the deck of *Terra Nova*, 1910–1912. *[A108/001500; SP4808]*

Sailors making clothing on the deck of *Terra Nova*, 1910–1912. *[A108/001504; SP4812]*

Lieutenant Rennick at the sounding machine on board *Terra Nova*, 1910–1912. *[A108/001506; SP4814]*

McCarthy at the wheel. "Wolsey underwear," 1911. *[A108/001517; SP4825]*

F. Drake taking meteorological observations, 1910–1912. *[A108/001536; SP4844]*

Lieutenant Rennick cuts Lillie's hair (off New Zealand), 1910–1912. *[A108/001541; SP4849]*

Portrait of Jas. Denistoun on the deck of *Terra Nova*, 1910–1912. *[A108/001542; SP4850]*

Meares and dogs on the ice house, January 3, 1911. *[A108/000806; SP4114]*

Sunset off New Zealand, March 30, 1912. *[A108/001547; SP4855]*

Outdoor Life at Cape Evans

Lieutenant Evans washing at the pool, January 7, 1911. *[A108/000845; SP4153]*

Evans and Nelson making an ice cave, January 12, 1911. *[A108/000857; SP4165]*

Mt. Erebus from the ship; sledge and ballast in foreground, January 13, 1911. *[A108/000859; SP4167]*

Berg aground near Cape Evans. Boat coming off. *Terra Nova* aground, January 20, 1911. *[A108/000875; SP4183]*

Stacking patent fuel, January 23, 1911. *[A108/000880; SP4188]*

Interest in the trawl catch, January 24, 1911. *[A108/000881; SP4189]*

Wolsey underwear, February 7, 1911. *[A108/000885; SP4193]*

Mandelberg windproofs, February 7, 1911. *[A108/000886; SP4194]*

Sledging and a cup of Fry's, February 7, 1911. *[A108/000888; SP4196]*

Lieutenant Rennick with artificial horizon, February 9, 1911. *[A108/000894; SP4202]*

Ponting and Lashly with a squid found by Ponting at Cape Royds, February 16, 1911. *[A108/000918; SP4226]*

Nelson attaching townet to kite, March 15, 1911. *[A108/000959; SP4267]*

Nelson and Day landing the townet, March 15, 1911. *[A108/000960; SP4268]*

Doctor Wilson and Bowers reading the Ramp thermometer, June 7, 1911. *[A108/001021; SP4329]*

Day digging out the snow by motors, August 1, 1911. *[A108/001039; SP4347]*

C. S. Wright working at night with the transit, August 8, 1911. *[A108/001040; SP4348]*

Captain Scott, Simpson, Bowers, and Evans leaving, September 15, 1911. *[A108/001051; SP4359]*

Lieutenant Evans and one of the sledging theodolites (Barne Glacier in background), October 1911. *[A108/001091; SP4399]*

Lieutenant Evans surveying, October 1911. *[A108/001092; SP4400]*

Silt bands in Barne Glacier and Lieutenant Gran, October 1911. *[A108/001102; SP4410]*

Lieut. T. Gran turning on skis, October 1911. *[A108/001104; SP4412]*

Day and Hooper on return from the Barrier, December 21, 1911. *[A108/001183; SP4491]*

Nelson's igloo and sledge, December 24, 1911. *[A108/001188; SP4496]*

Nelson in igloo with water bottle (Nansen-Pettersson insulating), December 24, 1911. *[A108/001189; SP4497]*

Nelson with reversing thermometers, December 24, 1911. *[A108/001191; SP4499]*

Return of Atkinson's party, January 29, 1912. *[A108/001237; SP4545]*

Demetri and some of the dogs, 1912. *[A108/001259; SP4567]*

Lieutenant Pennell and prismatic compass in the pack, December 1910. *[A108/001289; SP4597]*

The whale boat off Cape Crozier, January 1911. *[A108/001309; SP4617]*

Mt. Erebus from the *Terra Nova* at the ice foot, January 1911. *[A108/001314; SP4622]*

Doctor Simpson entering the magnetic hut, March 1911. *[A108/001326; SP4634]*

Doctor Simpson inflating one of his balloons, April 7, 1911. *[A108/001330; SP4638]*

Doctor Wilson at the sunshine recorder, August 26, 1911. *[A108/001334; SP4642]*

C. H. Meares cutting up seal meat for the dogs, November 1911. *[A108/001356; SP4664]*

Heinz advertisement, January 9, 1911. *[A108/001421; SP4729]*

Hooper and Demetri with a seal, 1910–1912. *[A108/001475; SP4783]*

Watering the ship at Glacier Tongue, 1911. *[A108/001514; SP4822]*

Ernest Shackleton's hut, February 17, 1911. *[A108/000921; SP4229]*

The first warm sunny spring day (−15°F). Hut and Mt. Erebus, September 17, 1911. *[A108/001059; SP4367]*

Shackleton's hut and Mt. Erebus, November 27, 1911. *[A108/001151; SP4459]*

First appearance of the sun over the Barne Glacier. Hut in foreground, August 25, 1911. *[A108/001329; SP4637]*

First rays of sunshine on the hut and some fellows watching it, August 26, 1911. *[A108/001333; SP4641]*

Getting one of the motors on to the sea ice, October 1911. *[A108/001096; SP4404]*

Day and one of the motors. Mt. Erebus in the background, October 1911. *[A108/001097; SP4405]*

The motor party: Lieutenant Evans, Day, Lashly, and Hooper by one of the motors, October 1911. *[A108/001100; SP4408]*

Day and Lashly fixing up one of the motors for the start of the Southern Journey, November 1911. *[A108/001361; SP4669]*

Day, Nelson, and Lashly probing a crevasse on the Barne Glacier, February 21, 1911. *[A108/000926; SP4234]*

Demetri and his dog team, 1912. *[A108/001260; SP4568]*

Captain Scott, Doctor Simpson, Lieutenant Bowers, and Evans leaving the hut for the west. Going on to the sea ice, September 15, 1911. *[A108/001337; SP4645]*

Indoor Life at Cape Evans

Nelson, Day, and Lashly in Shackleton's hut, February 17, 1911. *[A108/000922; SP4230]*

Interior of darkroom, March 24, 1911. *[A108/000968; SP4276]*

Taylor, Debenham, and Gran in cubicle, May 18, 1911. *[A108/001001; SP4309]*

Doctor Wilson working up a sketch, May 19, 1911. *[A108/001003; SP4311]*

A. C. Cherry-Garrard and his typewriter, June 8, 1911. *[A108/001024; SP4332]*

Midwinter Day tree, June 22, 1911. *[A108/001027; SP4336]*

Seaman Evans dressing Doctor Atkinson's frostbitten hand, July 6, 1911. *[A108/001032; SP4340]*

C. H. Meares making a dog harness, July 19, 1911. *[A108/001036; SP4344]*

Evans, Ford, and Crean putting a sledge together, August 30, 1911. *[A108/001044; SP4352]*

C. H. Meares and Demetri by the blubber stove in the *Discovery* hut, November 3, 1911. *[A108/001109; SP4417]*

Doctor Simpson in his lab, December 21, 1911. *[A108/001182; SP4490]*

Doctor Simpson at work in the magnetic hut, January 5, 1912. *[A108/001203; SP4511]*

Doctor Simpson at work in the magnetic hut, January 1912. *[A108/001204; SP4512]*

Doctor Simpson at the cloud chart, January 1912. *[A108/001205; SP4513]*

Packing sugar for sledging rations, January 1912. *[A108/001230; SP4538]*

The cook Clissold making pies, January 1912. *[A108/001239; SP4547]*

Hair cutting: Anton and P. Keohane, January 1912. *[A108/001240; SP4548]*

Dyne's anemometer in Simpson's lab registering 50 miles (80 km) an hour, 1912. *[A108/001253; SP4561]*

Portraits

Some of the *Terra Nova* crew on the fo'c'sle, December 28, 1910. *[A108/000776; SP4084]*

F. E. Debenham, April 13, 1911. *[A108/000983; SP4291]*

Lieutenant Bowers, April 13, 1911. *[A108/000984; SP4292]*

C. H. Meares and dog Osman, August 28, 1911. *[A108/001042; SP4350]*

A. C. Cherry-Garrard, November 1911. *[A108/001344; SP4652]*

Captain Scott at the ice crack, October 8, 1911. *[A108/001067; SP4375]*

Clissold on the Matterhorn Berg, October 8, 1911. *[A108/001075; SP4382]*

Ponting on the Matterhorn Berg, October 8, 1911. *[A108/001076; SP4384]*

Lieutenant Gran at Glacier Tongue, January 1911. *[A108/001512; SP4820]*

Full length portrait of Doctor Wilson standing at the door of the hut, October 1911. *[A108/001106; SP4414]*

Captain Oates, January 1912. *[A108/001242; SP4550]*

Doctor Atkinson, October 1911. *[A108/001108; SP4416]*

Lieutenant Evans by the motor, November 1911. *[A108/001336; SP4644]*

C. S. Wright, November 1911. *[A108/001340; SP4648]*

Seaman Crean, November 1911. *[A108/001345; SP4653]*

Seaman Keohane, November 1911. *[A108/001346; SP4654]*

Seaman Forde, November 1911. *[A108/001347; SP4655]*

Petty Officer Evans, November 1911. *[A108/001352; SP4660]*

Mechanic Lashly, November 1911. *[A108/001354; SP4662]*

B. C. Day by the motor, November 1911. *[A108/001343; SP4651]*

Antarctic Animals

Skua gull and chick, January 6, 1911. *[A108/000834; SP4142]*

Skua gull feeding chick, January 6, 1911. *[A108/000837; SP4145]*

Skua's nest and eggs, January 1912. *[A108/001210; SP4518]*

Skua settling on eggs, January 1912. *[A108/001215; SP4523]*

Young (three-day) chicks in nest, January 1912. *[A108/001223; SP4531]*

Sooty albatross on the wing, 1910–1912. *[A108/001533; SP4841]*

Weddell seal diving off the ice. Cape Evans, March 15, 1911. *[A108/000965; SP4273]*

Young Weddell seal, November 9, 1911. *[A108/001128; SP4436]*

Weddell seal and calf at Razorback, November 9, 1911. *[A108/0001129; SP4437]*

Seal coming up to breathe, November 19, 1911. *[A108/001138; SP4446]*

Seal with calf, November 19, 1911. *[A108/001142; SP4450]*

Seals at Razorback, November 19, 1911. *[A108/001145; SP4453]*

Killer whales off Barne Glacier, 1912. *[A108/001262; SP4570]*

Penguins and an iceberg, January 7, 1911. *[A108/000839; SP4147]*

Mt. Erebus from ice foot with penguins in foreground, January 13, 1911. *[A108/000861; SP4169]*

Rennick and Drake making friendly advances to Adélie penguins, February 9, 1911. *[A108/000895; SP4203]*

Rennick and a friendly Adélie penguin, February 9, 1911. *[A108/000898; SP4206]*

A corner of the penguinery at Cape Royds, February 13, 1911. *[A108/000907; SP4215]*

Penguins and a berg at Cape Royds, February 13, 1911. *[A108/000910; SP4218]*

On the penguinery, Cape Royds, November 26, 1911. *[A108/001157; SP4465]*

Adélie penguins love-making, December 8, 1911. *[A108/001171; SP4479]*

Herbert Ponting on the penguinery. Cape Royds, November 1911. *[A108/001365; SP4673]*

Angry penguin attacking Herbert Ponting. Cape Royds, November 1911. *[A108/001369; SP4677]*

Ecstatic Adélie penguin, November 1911. *[A108/001377; SP4685]*

Adélie penguin: attitude study, November 1911. *[A108/001378; SP4686]*

Adélie penguin: attitude study, November 1911. *[A108/001395; SP4703]*

Clissold and an Emperor penguin, 1910–1912. *[A108/001488; SP4796]*

Some of the ponies on *Terra Nova*, 1910–1912. *[A108/000786; SP4094]*

Captain Oates and pony Snippets, October 1911. *[A108/001085; SP4393]*

Lieutenant Bowers and pony Victor, October 1911. *[A108/001086; SP4394]*

Seaman Crean and pony Bones, October 1911. *[A108/001087; SP4395]*

Seaman Keohane and pony Jimmy Pig, October 1911. *[A108/001089; SP4397]*

C. S. Wright and pony Chinaman, 1910–1912. *[A108/001425; SP4733]*

Husky Hohol, 1910–1912. *[A108/001427; SP4735]*

Husky Lappy, 1910–1912. *[A108/001428; SP4736]*

Husky Wolk, 1910–1912. *[A108/001431; SP4739]*

Husky Julik, 1910–1912. *[A108/001439; SP4747]*

Husky Brodiaga, 1910–1912. *[A108/001440; SP4748]*

Husky Osman, 1910–1912. *[A108/001467; SP4775]*

Husky Koomagai, 1910–1912. *[A108/001470; SP4778]*

Landscapes

A large tabular berg, December 9, 1910. *[A108/000749; SP4057]*

Detail of the pack, December 11, 1910. *[A108/000755; SP4063]*

Telephoto of tilted barrier berg, December 18, 1910. *[A108/000764; SP4072]*

Telephoto. Large berg in pack, December 20, 1910. *[A108/000767; SP4075]*

Young pancake ice forming at West Beach. Mt. Erebus in background, March 9, 1911. *[A108/000956; SP4264]*

Lead opening and shadow of bowsprit, December 28, 1910. *[A108/000778; SP4086]*

In the pack. Sky reflection, December 28, 1910. *[A108/000781; SP4089]*

Ross Sea. Open water and clouds, about 11:00 a.m., January 2, 1911. *[A108/000803; SP4111]*

End of the Barrier, January 3, 1911. *[A108/000812; SP4120]*

Glacier breaking away off the Cape Crozier penguin rookery, January 3, 1911. *[A108/000814; SP4122]*

Mt. Erebus at 7:00 p.m., January 3, 1911. *[A108/000818; SP4126]*

Mt. Erebus at 1:15 a.m., January 4, 1911. *[A108/000823; SP4131]*

Mt. Erebus at 1:30 a.m., January 4, 1911. *[A108/000823; SP4132]*

An Antarctic cascade near the house, January 7, 1911. *[A108/000842; SP4150]*

Skua gulls on the floe, January 9, 1911. *[A108/000852; SP4160]*

Mt. Erebus from the ship, sledges on ice, and light effect on the snow, January 13, 1911. *[A108/000858; SP4166]*

Mt. Erebus's summit, January 13, 1911. *[A108/000863; SP4171]*

Cloud effect at Cape Royds and berg, February 15, 1911. *[A108/000913; SP4221]*

Cape Royds looking north, February 15, 1911. *[A108/000914; SP4222]*

Cape Royds looking south, February 15, 1911. *[A108/000915; SP4223]*

Mt. Erebus from West Beach at 5:00 p.m., March 7, 1911. *[A108/000942; SP4250]*

Bergs and floe off Cape Evans, March 7, 1911. *[A108/000945; SP4253]*

North Beach, camp, and Mt. Erebus from the west, March 7, 1911. *[A108/000946; SP4254]*

Young pancake ice forming at West Beach. Mt. Erebus in background, March 9, 1911. *[A108/000955; SP4263]*

Pancake ice forming on sea, March 9, 1911. *[A108/000957; SP4265]*

North Bay and camp from the east, March 16, 1911. *[A108/000966; SP4274]*

Sun rising behind Mt. Erebus at 9:30 a.m., March 29, 1911. *[A108/000976; SP4284]*

Mirage of Cape Barne and glacier, March 16, 1911. *[A108/000979; SP4287]*

Land's End and adjoining glacier, April 28, 1911. *[A108/000992; SP4300]*

Entrance to Land's End Glacier. Captain Scott, April 28, 1911. *[A108/000995; SP4303]*

Looking to Tent Island from one of the caves. Captain Scott and Wright, April 28, 1911. *[A108/000997; SP4305]*

Telephoto of smoke from Mt. Erebus 10:00 a.m., September 9, 1911. *[A108/001048; SP4356]*

The point of the Barne Glacier (where it turns round to the Bay before Cape Barne), September 18, 1911. *[A108/001061; SP4369]*

Mt. Erebus across the ice crack, October 8, 1911. *[A108/001070; SP4378]*

The face of the Matterhorn Berg (just before Clissold fell), October 8, 1911. *[A108/001074; SP4383]*

Discovery hut and the gap, November 4, 1911. *[A108/001110; SP4418]*

The Vince Cross at Hut Point and Mt. Discovery in the distance (and nice sky effect), November 4, 1911. *[A108/001111; SP4419]*

Castle Rock, November 5, 1911. *[A108/001118; SP4426]*

Mt. Erebus and berg as we floated off. 4:45 p.m., January 20, 1911. *[A108/000874; SP4182]*

Mt. Erebus and Back Door Bay, Cape Royds, November 27, 1911. *[A108/001152; SP4460]*

Adélie penguin track and sledge track crossing, December 8, 1911. *[A108/001170; SP4478]*

Cumulus cloud over the Barne Glacier, December 2, 1911. *[A108/001173; SP4481]*

Approaching snow storm, about 3:00 p.m., December 18, 1911. *[A108/001174; SP4482]*

Barne Glacier and cloud effect, December 1911. *[A108/001175; SP4483]*

Beautiful cirrus clouds over Barne Glacier, December 19, 1911. *[A108/001181; SP4489]*

Telephoto of Church Berg, seals, and Western Mountains from Vane Hill, December 27, 1911. *[A108/001196; SP4504]*

Church Berg and seals, December 29, 1911. *[A108/001197; SP4505]*

Hut and Western Mountains, January 1912. *[A108/001226; SP4534]*

Turk's Head from Glacier Front, January 1912. *[A108/001227; SP4535]*

Front of Turk's Head Glacier looking north, January 1912. *[A108/001229; SP4537]*

Ice breaking up off Cape Evans, January 30, 1912. *[A108/001233; SP4541]*

Iridescent clouds over Barne Glacier, 1912. *[A108/001254; SP4562]*

Cloud effect over Barne Glacier, 1912. *[A108/001255; SP4563]*

Hut Point and Observation Hill from *Terra Nova*, March 4, 1912. *[A108/001274; SP4582]*

Curious clouds and earth shadow on Mt. Erebus, 9:45 a.m., March 26, 1911. *[A108/001321; SP4629]*

The gallery shows examples of the photographs taken by Herbert Ponting on Scott's *Terra Nova* Expedition, 1910–1913. In many cases, the archive at the Royal Geographical Society contains several similar pictures within each category. In addition to those illustrated on pages 226–235, others on the same subjects are listed below.

The *Terra Nova*

Entering the pack. Fo'c'sle of the *Terra Nova*, December 9, 1910. [A108/000746; SP4054]

The *Terra Nova* held up for the first time in the ice, December 11, 1910. [A108/000753; SP4061]

The *Terra Nova* held up in the pack, December 13, 1910. [A108/000757; SP4065]

The *Terra Nova* held up in the pack, December 13, 1910. [A108/000758; SP4067]

The *Terra Nova* held up in the pack. Ice point in the foreground, December 13, 1910. [A108/000761; SP4069]

The *Terra Nova* held up in the pack. Ice point in the foreground, December 13, 1910. [A108/000762; SP4070]

The *Terra Nova* held up in the pack, December 13, 1910. [A108/000763; SP4071]

The prow of the *Terra Nova* opening the pack, December 19, 1910. [A108/000765; SP4073]

Surgeon Levick skinning a penguin on the *Terra Nova*, 1910–1912. [A108/000784; SP4092]

Lillie getting a townet out, January 1, 1911. [A108/000793; SP4101]

Nelson sending down the water bottle, January 1, 1911. [A108/000796; SP4104]

Nelson and Lillie with water bottle closed, January 1, 1911. [A108/000797; SP4105]

Nelson and Lillie taking sample from bottle, January 1, 1911. [A108/000798; SP4106]

Ross Sea. Cloud effect at 7:00 p.m. Ship's rail in foreground, January 2, 1911. [A108/000804; SP4112]

The *Terra Nova* and a berg at ice foot, January 16, 1911. [A108/000871; SP4179]

Lillie and Levick examining the trawl catch, January 24, 1911. [A108/000882; SP4190]

The *Terra Nova* lying off Barne Glacier, February 8, 1911. [A108/000890; SP4198]

The *Terra Nova* lying off the shore from the hut, February 8, 1911. [A108/000891; SP4199]

The last boat for the ship, February 9, 1911. [A108/000900; SP4208]

Lillie with a large glass sponge, 1912. [A108/001272; SP4580]

Terra Nova at ice foot off Hut Point, 1912. [A108/001276; SP4584]

Doctor Levick skinning a penguin on the *Terra Nova*, December 1910. [A108/001290; SP4598]

Doctor Levick skinning a penguin on the *Terra Nova*, December 1910. [A108/001292; SP4600]

The *Terra Nova* at the ice foot off Cape Evans, January 1911. [A108/001307; SP4615]

The *Terra Nova* at Glacier Tongue, January 1911. [A108/001315; SP4623]

Captain Scott and Lieutenant Evans on the deck of the *Terra Nova*, December 1910. [A108/001499; SP4807]

On *Terra Nova* "at the pumps," December 1910. [A108/001502; SP4810]

F. Drake reading the compass on the deck of the *Terra Nova*, 1910–1912. [A108/001505; SP4813]

F. Drake taking the temperature of the sea on board *Terra Nova*, 1910–1912. [A108/001507; SP4815]

Lieutenant Evans entering the crow's nest of *Terra Nova*, 1910–1912. [A108/001522; SP4830]

F. Drake taking meteorological observations, 1910–1912. [A108/001535; SP4843]

F. Drake on the deck of the *Terra Nova*, 1910–1912. [A108/001537; SP4845]

Mr. Williams at the sounding engine on the deck of the *Terra Nova*, 1910–1912. [A108/001538; SP4846]

Herbert Ponting cinematographing a heavy gale from the bridge of the *Terra Nova*, 1910–1912. [A108/001540; SP4848]

Portrait of Lieutenant Rennick on the deck of *Terra Nova* (off New Zealand), 1910–1912. [A108/001543; SP4851]

Group on the fo'c'sle off New Zealand (deck of *Terra Nova*), 1910–1912. [A108/001544; SP4852]

Portrait of Lieutenant Rennick on the deck of *Terra Nova* (off New Zealand), 1910–1912. [A108/001545; SP4853]

Group on the fo'c'sle off New Zealand, 1910–1912. [A108/001546; SP4854]

Outdoor Life at Cape Evans

Doctor Wilson skinning a seal on the ice, January 7, 1911. [A108/000846; SP4154]

Drake, a member of the crew, pulls sledge carrying blocks of ice to melt for drinking water, January 10, 1911. [A108/000856; SP4164]

Mather and sledge of ballast, January 14, 1911. [A108/000864; SP4172]

Piling stores near hut. Colman's flour, January 23, 1911. [A108/000879; SP4187]

Rennick and Drake making friendly advances to Adélie penguins, February 9, 1911. [A108/000896; SP4204]

Rennick and Drake making friendly advances to Adélie penguins, February 9, 1911. [A108/000897; SP4205]

The whaler leaving for the *Terra Nova*, February 9, 1911. [A108/000899; SP4207]

Left behind in Victoria Land, February 9, 1911. [A108/000901; SP4209]

Packing a sledge at the top of the moraine for a trip to Shackleton's, February 11, 1911. [A108/000903; SP4211]

Packing a sledge at the top of the moraine for a trip to Shackelton's, February 11, 1911. [A108/000904; SP4212]

Day, Nelson, and Lashly staking out the Barne Glacier, February 11, 1911. [A108/000905; SP4213]

Cape Royds from the glacier between Cape Barne and Royds, February 11, 1911. [A108/000906; SP4214]

Day and Nelson on Clear Lake. Cape Royds, February 15, 1911. [A108/000916; SP4224]

Day and Nelson on Clear Lake. Cape Royds, February 15, 1911. [A108/000917; SP4225]

Ernest Shackleton's hut, February 17, 1911. [A108/000921; SP4229]

Day, Nelson, Lashly, and sledge on Barne Glacier, February 21, 1911. [A108/000924; SP4232]

Day, Nelson, and Lashly among crevasses on Barne Glacier, February 21, 1911. [A108/000927; SP4235]

Entrance to cave in Land's End Glacier with Wright, April 28, 1911. [A108/000994; SP4302]

Looking to Tent Island from one of the caves. Captain Scott and Wright, April 28, 1911. [A108/000998; SP4306]

Doctor Atkinson and Clissold taking in the fish trap (−40°F), May 28, 1911. [A108/001012; SP4320]

Doctor Wilson, Cherry-Garrard, and Forde with a sea leopard on a sledge, May 28, 1911. [A108/001015; SP4323]

Oates and Meares on skis, June 4, 1911. [A108/001017; SP4325]

Ponting cutting a hole in the ice for lowering the fish trap, June 26, 1911. [A108/001029; SP4337]

F. Debenham and weathered Kenyte, September 9, 1911. [A108/001050; SP4358]

A blizzard beginning on Mt. Erebus, October 1, 1911. [A108/001062; SP4370]

Clissold and his dog sledge, October 1, 1911. [A108/001063; SP4371]

Day and the motor garage, October 5, 1911. [A108/001064; SP4372]

Day and the motor garage, October 5, 1911. [A108/001065; SP4373]

Harnessing Michael to the sledge, October 1911. [A108/001090; SP4398]

A motor leaving the winter "garage," October 1911. [A108/001094; SP4402]

Getting one of the motors on to the sea ice, October 1911. [A108/001095; SP4403]

Day and one of the motors, October 1911. [A108/001098; SP4406]

Loaded sledges for one of the motors on the sea ice, October 1911. [A108/001099; SP4407]

Lieut. T. Gran on skis, October 1911. [A108/001103; SP4411]

Demetri's dogs (with Demetri) ready to start south, November 5, 1911. [A108/001115; SP4423]

C. H. Meares and Demetri with their dog teams ready to start south, November 5, 1911. [A108/001116; SP4424]

C. H. Meares and Demetri with their dog teams southward bound from Hut Point, November 5, 1911. [A108/001117; SP4425]

Ponting and Nelson camped by the penguinery, Cape Royds, November 27, 1911. [A108/001153; SP4461]

Herbert Ponting and photo go-cart with dogs, Mass Johnson and Lassie, December 24, 1911. [A108/001186; SP4494]

Nelson letting down the water bottle, December 24, 1911. [A108/001190; SP4498]

Nelson with thermometers reversed, December 24, 1911. [A108/001192; SP4500]

Return of Atkinson's party, January 29, 1912. [A108/001237; SP4545]

Return of Atkinson's party, January 29, 1912. [A108/001238; SP4546]

Doctor Atkinson's dog team landing stores from ship, 1912. [A108/001258; SP4566]

A party landing stores from the ship, 1912. [A108/001261; SP4569]

Boat going to the hut from the ship 3:00 a.m., March 4, 1912. [A108/001278; SP4586]

Nelson and Priestley making a hole in a floe, December 1910. [A108/001287; SP4595]

Doctor Wilson loading the whale gun, December 1910. [A108/001296; SP4604]

Captain Oates and Seaman Abbott picketing ponies, January 1911. [A108/001310; SP4618]

Watering the *Terra Nova* at Glacier Tongue, January 1911. [A108/001316; SP4624]

Doctor Simpson leaving the magnetograph ice cave, March 1911. [A108/001325; SP4633]

Doctor Simpson taking observations on Vane Hill; B. Day and balloon theodolite, March 16, 1911. [A108/001328; SP4636]

Doctor Wilson watching the record receiving the Sun's first rays of the season, August 26, 1911. [A108/001332; SP4640]

Captain Scott, Doctor Simpson, Lieutenant Bowers, and Evans leaving the hut for the west, September 15, 1911. [A108/001339; SP4647]

Wright and Bowers packing sledges for the Southern Journey, November 1911. [A108/001358; SP4666]

Ponting making a hole in the ice, June 26, 1911. [A108/001519; SP4827]

Indoor Life at Cape Evans

Interior of darkroom, March 24, 1911. [A108/000969; SP4277]

Interior of darkroom: the sink, March 24, 1911. [A108/000970; SP4278]

Nelson's and Day's bunks, March 25, 1911. [A108/000971; SP4279]

Ponting's bed in darkroom, March 25, 1911. [A108/000972; SP4280]

Simpson's laboratory, March 31, 1911. [A108/000978; SP4286]

Evans and Crean mending sleeping bags, May 16, 1911. [A108/000999; SP4307]

Doctor Wilson working up a sketch, May 18, 1911. [A108/001002; SP4310]

Taylor and Debenham in cubicle, May 19, 1911. [A108/001004; SP4312]

Anton cooking mashes in the stable, May 23, 1911. [A108/001007; SP4315]

Meares and Oates at the blubber stove, May 26, 1911. [A108/001011; SP4319]

A winter work group, June 6, 1911. [A108/001020; SP4328]

Midwinter work group, June 8, 1911. [A108/001023; SP4331]

Midwinter Day Dinner, June 22, 1911. [A108/001026; SP4334]

The gas plant, December 20, 1911. [A108/001179; SP4487]

The gas plant, December 20, 1911. [A108/001180; SP4488]

Portraits

Captain Scott, just before leaving for the Southern Journey, January 26, 1911. [A108/000883; SP4191]

Evans and Crean, April 13, 1911. [A108/000989; SP4297]

Dr. E. A. Wilson, April 21, 1911. [A108/000991; SP4299]

Doctor Atkinson's frostbitten hand, July 5, 1911. [A108/001031; SP4339]

Captain Oates at the stable door, August 30, 1911. [A108/001046; SP4353]

Captain Scott at the ice crack, October 8, 1911. [A108/001068; SP4376]

Portrait of Lieutenant Bowers, October 11, 1911. [A108/001079; SP4387]

Captain Scott on skis, October 1911. [A108/001093; SP4401]

Western Geological Party: F. Debenham, T. G. Taylor, T. Gran, and Forde, 1912. [A108/001269; SP4577]

Western Geological Party: F. Debenham, T. G. Taylor, T. Gran, and Forde, 1912. [A108/001270; SP4578]

Group of officers of *Terra Nova*, 1912. [A108/001282; SP4590]

C. H. Meares and dog Osman, August 26, 1911. [A108/001335; SP4643]

C. S. Wright, November 1911. [A108/001341; SP4649]

B. C. Day by the motor, November 1911. [A108/001342; SP4650]

Seaman Forde, November 1911. [A108/001348; SP4656]

Petty Officer Evans, November 1911. [A108/001349; SP4657]

Petty Officer Evans, November 1911. [A108/001350; SP4658]

Petty Officer Evans, November 1911. [A108/001351; SP4659]

Mechanic Lashly, November 1911. [A108/001353; SP4661]

Steward Hooper, November 1911. [A108/001355; SP4663]

Lieutenant Evans at Glacier Tongue, January 1911. [A108/001510; SP4818]

Lieutenant Evans at Glacier Tongue, January 1911. [A108/001511; SP4819]

Lieutenant Bowers at Glacier Tongue, January 1911. [A108/001513; SP4821]

Emperor penguin's eggs, January 1912. [A108/001244; SP4552]

A Notothenia, 1912. [A108/001245; SP4553]

Sledging rations for one man for one day, 1912. [A108/001246; SP4554]

Finnesko (boots), 1912. [A108/001247; SP4555]

Ski shoes for finnesko (boots), 1912. [A108/001248; SP4556]

Ski adaptation for finnesko (boots), 1912. [A108/001249; SP4557]

Crampons for finnesko (boots), 1912. [A108/001250; SP4558]

Antarctic Animals

Penguins on the floe, December 24, 1910. [A108/000773; SP4081]

Penguins resting, January 7, 1911. [A108/000840; SP4148]

Penguins resting, January 7, 1911. [A108/000841; SP4149]

Sky effect (midnight Sun) and penguins at ice edge, January 13, 1911. [A108/000862; SP4170]

Adélie penguins "porpoising," January 15, 1911. [A108/000866; SP4174]

Adélie penguins "porpoising," January 15, 1911. [A108/000867; SP4175]

Penguins making for the water, January 16, 1911. [A108/000870; SP4178]

Penguins and a berg at Cape Royds, February 13, 1911. [A108/000908; SP4216]

Penguins and a berg at Cape Royds, February 13, 1911. [A108/000909; SP4217]

Group of young penguins. Cape Royds, February 14, 1911. [A108/000911; SP4219]

Moulting penguin, February 18, 1911. [A108/000923; SP4231]

On the penguinery. Cape Royds, November 26, 1911. [A108/001155; SP4463]

On the penguinery. Cape Royds, November 26, 1911. [A108/001156; SP4464]

On the penguinery. Cape Royds, November 26, 1911. [A108/001157; SP4465]

The penguinery after a blizzard. Cape Royds, December 8, 1911. [A108/001158; SP4466]

The penguinery after a blizzard. Cape Royds, December 8, 1911. [A108/001159; SP4467]

The penguinery after a blizzard. Cape Royds, December 8, 1911. [A108/001160; SP4468]

Penguins snowed up, December 8, 1911. [A108/001161; SP4469]

On the penguinery after a blizzard, December 8, 1911. [A108/001162; SP4470]

Sitting penguin snowed up, only head showing, December 8, 1911. [A108/001163; SP4471]

Sitting penguin snowed up, only head showing, December 8, 1911. [A108/001164; SP4472]

Sitting penguin snowed up, December 8, 1911. [A108/001165; SP4473]

Sitting penguin snowed up, December 8, 1911. [A108/001166; SP4474]

Sitting penguin snowed up, only head and tail showing, December 8, 1911. [A108/001167; SP4475]

Penguin spread-eagled, December 8, 1911. [A108/001168; SP4476]

The penguinery after the blizzard with Mt. Erebus behind, December 8, 1911. [A108/001169; SP4477]

Adélie penguins: a heated argument, December 8, 1911. [A108/001172; SP4480]

E. W. Nelson on the penguinery. Cape Royds, November 1911. [A108/001364; SP4672]

Herbert Ponting stroking a penguin on a nest. Cape Royds, November 1911. [A108/001366; SP4674]

Herbert Ponting stroking a penguin on a nest. Cape Royds, November 1911. [A108/001367; SP4675]

Angry penguin attacking Herbert Ponting, November 1911. [A108/001368; SP4676]

Adélie's snug nest amid rocks, November 1911. [A108/001370; SP4678]

Adélie's snug nest amid rocks, November 1911. [A108/001371; SP4679]

Some Adélie penguin nests are mounds of stones, November 1911. [A108/001372; SP4680]

"Ecstatic" Adélie penguin on nest, November 1911. [A108/001373; SP4681]

Other Adélie nests have no stones at all, November 1911. [A108/001374; SP4682]

"Ecstatic" Adélie penguin, November 1911. [A108/001375; SP4683]

"Ecstatic" Adélie penguin with eggs, November 1911. [A108/001376; SP4684]

Adélie penguin: attitude study, November 1911. [A108/001379; SP4687]

Adélie penguin: attitude study, November 1911. [A108/001380; SP4688]

Adélie penguin: attitude study, November 1911. [A108/001381; SP4689]

Adélie penguin: attitude study, November 1911. [A108/001382; SP4690]

Adélie penguin: attitude study, November 1911. [A108/001383; SP4691]

Adélie penguin: attitude study, November 1911. [A108/001384; SP4692]

Adélie penguin: attitude study, November 1911. [A108/001385; SP4693]

Adélie penguin: attitude study, November 1911. [A108/001386; SP4694]

Adélie penguin: attitude study, November 1911. [A108/001387; SP4695]

Adélie penguin: attitude study, November 1911. [A108/001388; SP4696]

Adélie penguin: attitude study, November 1911. [A108/001389; SP4697]

Adélie penguin: attitude study, November 1911. [A108/001390; SP4698]

Adélie penguin: attitude study, November 1911. [A108/001391; SP4699]

Adélie penguin: attitude study, November 1911. [A108/001392; SP4700]

Adélie penguin: attitude study, November 1911. [A108/001393; SP4701]

Adélie penguin: attitude study, November 1911. [A108/001394; SP4702]

Adélie penguin: attitude study, November 1911. [A108/001396; SP4704]

Adélie penguin about to turn eggs, November 1911. [A108/001397; SP4705]

Adélie penguin turning eggs, November 1911. [A108/001398; SP4706]

Adélie penguin turning eggs, November 1911. [A108/001399; SP4707]

A discussion between three Adélie penguins, November 1911. [A108/001400; SP4708]

A discussion between three Adélie penguins grows hotter, November 1911. [A108/001401; SP4709]

A discussion between three Adélie penguins becomes still hotter, November 1911. [A108/001402; SP4710]

A discussion between three Adélie penguins becomes a nose-pulling contest, November 1911. [A108/001403; SP4711]

A discussion between three Adélie penguins ends by one party getting a good licking, November 1911. [A108/001404; SP4712]

Penguin advertisement for Lyle's syrup, November 1911. [A108/001406; SP4714]

Penguin and chicks, January 9, 1911. [A108/001407; SP4715]

Penguin and chicks, January 9, 1911. [A108/001408; SP4716]

Penguin and chicks, January 9, 1911. [A108/001409; SP4717]

Penguin and chicks, January 9, 1911. [A108/001410; SP4718]

Penguin and chicks, January 9, 1911. [A108/001411; SP4719]

Penguin and chicks, January 9, 1911. [A108/001412; SP4720]

Penguin and chicks, January 9, 1911. [A108/001413; SP4721]

Penguin and chicks, January 9, 1911. [A108/001414; SP4722]

Penguin and chicks, January 9, 1911. [A108/001415; SP4723]

Penguin and chicks, January 9, 1911. [A108/001416; SP4724]

Penguin and chicks, January 9, 1911. [A108/001417; SP4725]

Penguin and chicks, January 9, 1911. [A108/001418; SP4726]

Penguin and chicks, January 9, 1911. [A108/001419; SP4727]

Penguin and chicks, January 9, 1911. [A108/001420; SP4728]

Reflections, penguinery. Cape Royds, January 9, 1911. [A108/001422; SP4730]

Pair of Adélie penguins, 1910–1912. [A108/001479; SP4787]

Group of Adélies on sea ice, 1910–1912. [A108/001480; SP4788]

Adélie penguin just jumped on to a floe, 1910–1912. [A108/001481; SP4789]

Adélie penguin leaping out of the water, 1910–1912. [A108/001482; SP4790]

Adélie penguin feeding young, 1910–1912. [A108/001523; SP4831]

Adélie penguin and young begging for food, 1910–1912. [A108/001525; SP4833]

Adélie penguins tobogganing, 1910–1912. [A108/001526; SP4834]

Emperor penguins on the heavy pancake ice, 1912. [A108/001266; SP4574]

An Emperor penguin, 1910–1912. [A108/001484; SP4792]

An Emperor penguin, 1910–1912. [A108/001486; SP4794]

A skua gull, January 6, 1911. [A108/000828; SP4136]

Skua gulls, male and female, January 6, 1911. [A108/000829; SP4137]

Skua gull's eggs in nest, January 6, 1911. [A108/000830; SP4138]

Skua and chick, a few days old, January 6, 1911. [A108/000832; SP4140]

Skua gull and chick, January 6, 1911. [A108/000833; SP4141]

Skua gull and chick, January 6, 1911. [A108/000834; SP4142]

Skua chick about one week old, January 6, 1911. [A108/000835; SP4143]

Skua gull bringing food to chick, January 6, 1911. [A108/000836; SP4144]

Gulls by hole in skua lake and Mt. Erebus, December 19, 1911. [A108/001178; SP4486]

Skua's nest and situation, January 1912. [A108/001209; SP4517]

Skua by nest and eggs, January 1912. [A108/001211; SP4519]

Skua by nest and eggs, January 1912. [A108/001212; SP4520]

Skua returning to eggs, January 1912. [A108/001213; SP4521]

Skua returning to eggs, January 1912. [A108/001214; SP4522]

Skua settling on eggs, January 1912. [A108/001216; SP4524]

Skua sitting, January 1912. [A108/001217; SP4525]

Skua sitting, January 1912. [A108/001218; SP4526]

Skuas bathing in lake, January 1912. [A108/001219; SP4527]

Skuas bathing in lake, January 1912. [A108/001220; SP4528]

Skua by nest and chick, January 1912. [A108/001221; SP4529]

Skua by nest and chick, January 1912. [A108/001222; SP4530]

Skua gull waiting to steal penguin eggs, November 1911. [A108/001405; SP4713]

Skuas picking a seal skin, 1910–1912. [A108/001485; SP4793]

Cape pigeon flying, December 1910. [A108/001529; SP4837]

Cape pigeon flying, December 1910. [A108/001531; SP4839]

Albatrosses foraging astern of Terra Nova, 1910–1912. [A108/000791; SP4099]

Albatrosses foraging astern of Terra Nova, 1910–1912. [A108/000792; SP4100]

Albatrosses in wake of Terra Nova, December 1910. [A108/001532; SP4840]

Albatross on the wing, 1910–1912. [A108/001534; SP4842]

Seals basking on new floe off Cape Evans, March 7, 1911. [A108/000943; SP4251]

Seals basking on new floe off Cape Evans, March 7, 1911. [A108/000944; SP4252]

Weddell seal. Cape Evans, March 15, 1911. [A108/000962; SP4270]

Weddell seal. Cape Evans, March 15, 1911. [A108/000963; SP4271]

Weddell seal. Cape Evans, March 15, 1911. [A108/000964; SP4272]

Weddell seal and newly born calf at Razorback, November 9, 1911. [A108/001120; SP4428]

Newly born Weddell seal calf at Razorback, November 9, 1911. [A108/001121; SP4429]

Weddell seal suckling calf, November 9, 1911. [A108/001122; SP4430]

Weddell seal suckling calf, November 9, 1911. [A108/001123; SP4431]

Weddell seal suckling calf, November 9, 1911. [A108/001124; SP4432]

Weddell seal and calf at Razorback, November 9, 1911. [A108/001125; SP4433]

Weddell seal and calf at Razorback, November 9, 1911. [A108/001126; SP4434]

Weddell seal and calf at Razorback, November 9, 1911. [A108/001127; SP4435]

Weddell seal and calf at Razorback, November 9, 1911. [A108/001130; SP4438]

Weddell seal and calf at Razorback, November 9, 1911. [A108/001131; SP4439]

Weddell seal and calf at Razorback, November 9, 1911. [A108/001132; SP4440]

Weddell seal and calf at Razorback, November 9, 1911. [A108/001133; SP4441]

Weddell seal and calf at Razorback, November 9, 1911. [A108/001134; SP4442]

Weddell seal enraged with calf at Razorback, November 9, 1911. [A108/001135; SP4443]

Tide crack and seal hole at Razorback, November 19, 1911. [A108/001136; SP4444]

Seals, Mt. Erebus, and Razorback (south), November 19, 1911. [A108/001137; SP4445]

Seal getting out of hole, November 19, 1911. [A108/001139; SP4447]

Seal with two young calves, alarmed, November 19, 1911. [A108/001140; SP4448]

Seal with two calves, November 19, 1911. [A108/001141; SP4449]

Seal with calf, November 19, 1911. [A108/001143; SP4451]

Seal with calf, November 19, 1911. [A108/001144; SP4452]

Seals at Razorback, November 19, 1911. [A108/001146; SP4454]

Seal with two calves, November 19, 1911. [A108/001147; SP4455]

Seals lying by Church Berg. Precipice effect, December 29, 1911. [A108/001198; SP4506]

Front of Turk's Head Glacier looking north with seal, January 1912. *[A108/001228; SP4536]*

Seal rising among ice floes, 1910–1912. *[A108/001471; SP4779]*

Seal rising among ice floes, 1910–1912. *[A108/001472; SP4780]*

Weddell seal. Cape Evans, 1910–1912. *[A108/001473; SP4781]*

Weddell seal. Cape Evans, 1910–1912. *[A108/001474; SP4782]*

Weddell seal. Cape Evans, 1910–1912. *[A108/001477; SP4785]*

Weddell seal. Cape Evans, 1910–1912. *[A108/001478; SP4786]*

A seal in brash ice, 1910–1912. *[A108/001492; SP4800]*

A seal in brash ice, 1910–1912. *[A108/001493; SP4801]*

A seal in brash ice, 1910–1912. *[A108/001495; SP4803]*

Seal and two calves, 1910–1912. *[A108/001527; SP4835]*

Weddell seal at Cape Evans, 1910–1912. *[A108/001528; SP4836]*

Seal and two calves, 1910–1912. *[A108/001530; SP4838]*

A sea leopard, May 28, 1911. *[A108/001013; SP4321]*

Forde and sea leopard, May 28, 1911. *[A108/001014; SP4322]*

Some of the ponies on *Terra Nova,* 1910–1912. *[A108/000787; SP4095]*

Interior of stable, March 28, 1911. *[A108/000975; SP4283]*

Evans and Crean with ponies on the ice, May 30, 1911. *[A108/001016; SP4324]*

Doctor Wilson and pony Nobby, October 1911. *[A108/001080; SP4388]*

Doctor Wilson and pony Nobby, October 1911. *[A108/001081; SP4389]*

Mr. Cherry-Garrard and pony Michael, October 1911. *[A108/001083; SP4391]*

P. O. Evans and pony Snatcher, October 1911. *[A108/001088; SP4396]*

Ponies picketed on the sea ice, January 1911. *[A108/001312; SP4620]*

Doctor Wilson, Lieutenant Bowers, Cherry-Garrard, and ponies on the sea ice, October 6, 1911. *[A108/001338; SP4646]*

Head of pony Victor, November 1911. *[A108/001357; SP4665]*

Heads of ponies in stable, 1910–1912. *[A108/001424; SP4732]*

Heads of ponies in stable, 1910–1912. *[A108/001426; SP4734]*

Husky Wolk, 1910–1912. *[A108/001430; SP4738]*

Husky Wolk, 1910–1912. *[A108/001432; SP4740]*

Husky Kasoi, 1910–1912. *[A108/001434; SP4742]*

Husky Kasoi, 1910–1912. *[A108/001435; SP4743]*

Husky Vaida, 1910–1912. *[A108/001437; SP4745]*

Husky Vaida, 1910–1912. *[A108/001441; SP4749]*

Husky Vaida, 1910–1912. *[A108/001442; SP4750]*

Husky Vaida, 1910–1912. *[A108/001443; SP4751]*

Husky Vaida, 1910–1912. *[A108/001444; SP4752]*

Husky Vaida, 1910–1912. *[A108/001445; SP4753]*

Husky Stareek, 1910–1912. *[A108/001448; SP4756]*

Husky Stareek, 1910–1912. *[A108/001449; SP4757]*

Husky Stareek, 1910–1912. *[A108/001450; SP4758]*

Husky Ostrenos, 1910–1912. *[A108/001451; SP4759]*

Husky Ostrenos, 1910–1912. *[A108/001452; SP4760]*

Husky Krisravitsa, 1910–1912. *[A108/001457; SP4765]*

Husky Krisravitsa, 1910–1912. *[A108/001459; SP4767]*

Husky Krisravitsa, 1910–1912. *[A108/001461; SP4769]*

Husky Krisravitsa, 1910–1912. *[A108/001462; SP4770]*

Husky Krisravitsa, 1910–1912. *[A108/001463; SP4771]*

Husky Osman, 1910–1912. *[A108/001465; SP4773]*

Husky Osman, 1910–1912. *[A108/001466; SP4774]*

Husky Osman, 1910–1912. *[A108/001468; SP4776]*

Killer whale rising in hole in ice, 1912. *[A108/001263; SP4571]*

A rorqual off Glacier Tongue, 1910–1912. *[A108/001489; SP4797]*

A whale diving under the ice, 1910–1912. *[A108/001490; SP4798]*

A shark off New Zealand, 1910–1912. *[A108/001548; SP4856]*

The squid found by Ponting and captured by him and Lashly at Cape Royds, February 16, 1911. *[A108/000919; SP4227]*

Landscapes

Sunset effect, Antarctic Circle, December 8, 1910. *[A108/000745; SP4053]*

Detail of the pack, December 11, 1910. *[A108/000756; SP4064]*

Telephoto of tilted barrier berg, December 18, 1910. *[A108/000764; SP4072]*

The berg that resembled an island, December 19, 1910. *[A108/000766; SP4074]*

Telephoto. Berg in pack. Debenham and Taylor on the ice, December 20, 1910. *[A108/000768; SP4076]*

Light effect on pack, December 22, 1910. *[A108/000771; SP4079]*

Detail of floe and penguins, December 24, 1910. *[A108/000774; SP4082]*

A lead opening in the pack, December 28, 1910. *[A108/000777; SP4085]*

Pack breaking up, December 28, 1910. *[A108/000779; SP4087]*

Detail of pack with penguins, December 28, 1910. *[A108/000780; SP4088]*

Typical piece of floating ice, January 1, 1911. *[A108/000799; SP4107]*

Typical piece of floating ice, January 1, 1911. *[A108/000800; SP4108]*

Ross Sea. Open water and clouds. Noon, January 2, 1911. *[A108/000801; SP4109]*

Ross Sea. Open water and clouds. Noon, January 2, 1911. *[A108/000802; SP4110]*

Mt. Terror about noon, January 3, 1911. *[A108/000807; SP4115]*

Ice blink over the Barrier, January 3, 1911. *[A108/000808; SP4116]*

View of the Barrier at 1:45 p.m., January 3, 1911. *[A108/000809; SP4117]*

The Barrier and Mt. Terror, 2:00 p.m., January 3, 1911. *[A108/000810; SP4118]*

Cape Crozier. Precipes, January 3, 1911. *[A108/000813; SP4121]*

Killer whale off the penguin rookery, January 3, 1911. *[A108/000815; SP4123]*

Mt. Terror at 6:00 p.m., January 3, 1911. *[A108/000816; SP4124]*

Mt. Terror at 6.30 p.m., January 3, 1911. *[A108/000817; SP4125]*

Mt. Erebus at 11:00 p.m., January 3, 1911. *[A108/000819; SP4127]*

Mt. Bird at 11:00 p.m., January 3, 1911. *[A108/000821; SP4129]*

Mt. Erebus at 1:15 a.m., January 4, 1911. *[A108/000822; SP4130]*

Pool below cascade, January 7, 1911. *[A108/000843; SP4151]*

The cavern in the iceberg. *Terra Nova* in the distance, January 8, 1911. *[A108/000850; SP4158]*

Detail of sea ice breaking up, January 9, 1911. *[A108/000853; SP4161]*

Cumulus cloud on Barne Glacier, January 13, 1911. *[A108/000860; SP4168]*

Mt. Erebus and stranded berg. Made just when ship struck, January 20, 1911. *[A108/000873; SP4181]*

Stranded berg and boat coming off, January 20, 1911. *[A108/000876; SP4184]*

Mt. Erebus and whaling boat in foreground, January 20, 1911. *[A108/000877; SP4185]*

Ice showing morainic cones on Green Lake. Cape Royds, February 15, 1911. *[A108/000912; SP4220]*

Sastrugi on Barne Glacier, February 21, 1911. *[A108/000928; SP4236]*

Sastrugi on Barne Glacier, February 21, 1911. *[A108/000929; SP4237]*

Wave at West Beach, February 28, 1911. *[A108/000931; SP4239]*

Wave breaking at West Beach, February 28, 1911. *[A108/000934; SP4242]*

Wave breaking at West Beach, February 28, 1911. *[A108/000935; SP4243]*

Wave breaking at West Beach, February 28, 1911. *[A108/000936; SP4244]*

Wave breaking at West Beach, February 28, 1911. *[A108/000937; SP4245]*

Wave breaking at West Beach, February 28, 1911. *[A108/000938; SP4246]*

Cloud effect on Mt. Erebus at noon, March 7, 1911. *[A108/000939; SP4247]*

Mt. Erebus and dome cloud from West Beach, 2:30 p.m., icicled glacier in foreground, March 7, 1911. *[A108/000940; SP4248]*

Weathered Kenyte boulder near house, March 8, 1911. *[A108/000948; SP4256]*

Weathered Kenyte boulder near house. "The Antarcticossauras," March 8, 1911. *[A108/000949; SP4257]*

Weathered ice after blizzard at Cape Evans, looking to Castle Rock, March 8, 1911. *[A108/000950; SP4258]*

Spray ridges of ice, Cape Evans. Inaccessible Island in the distance, March 8, 1911. *[A108/000951; SP4259]*

Weathered ice furrows after a blizzard at Cape Evans and crevasse, looking south toward Turks Head, March 8, 1911. *[A108/000953; SP4261]*

Morainic cones, Mt. Erebus in background. Day on top, March 9, 1911. *[A108/000954; SP4262]*

"Frost smoke" on North Bay, March 13, 1911. *[A108/000958; SP4266]*

Clouds on Mt. Erebus, 8:45 a.m., March 26, 1911. *[A108/000973; SP4281]*

The Castle Berg with dog sledge, September 17, 1911. *[A108/001054; SP4362]*

Huge ice bastions of the Castle Berg (Clissold at base), September 17, 1911. *[A108/001055; SP4363]*

A great bastion of ice, September 17, 1911. *[A108/001057; SP4365]*

Under the lee of the Castle Berg, September 17, 1911. *[A108/001058; SP4366]*

The point of the Barne Glacier (where it turns round to the Bay before Cape Barne), September 18, 1911. *[A108/001060; SP4368]*

The Matterhorn Berg, profile (Clissold on summit), October 8, 1911. *[A108/001072; SP4380]*

Summit of Mt. Erebus, October 1911. *[A108/001107; SP4415]*

Hut Point and Vince Cross looking south, November 4, 1911. *[A108/001112; SP4420]*

A view of Hut Point, November 4, 1911. *[A108/001114; SP4422]*

Castle Rock, November 5, 1911. *[A108/001118; SP4426]*

Midnight Sun effect on Mt. Discovery taken from one mile south of Razorback at 11:00 p.m., November 5, 1911. *[A108/001119; SP4427]*

The pillar at Cape Barne, November 29, 1911. *[A108/001149; SP4457]*

Pinnacle of Church Berg and icicles with Anton, December 29, 1911. *[A108/001201; SP4510]*

Telephoto, Mt. Discovery, 1912. *[A108/001225; SP4533]*

Ice breaking up off Cape Evans, January 30, 1912. *[A108/001234; SP4542]*

Cloud effect over Barne Glacier, 1912. *[A108/001256; SP4564]*

Cloud effect over Barne Glacier, 1912. *[A108/001257; SP4565]*

Heavy pancake ice (several feet thick in layers) in which ship was held whilst trying to rescue the Northern Party, 1912. *[A108/001264; SP4572]*

Heavy pancake ice with floes, 1912. *[A108/001267; SP4575]*

Frost smoke off Glacier Tongue, 1912. *[A108/001273; SP4581]*

Wake of *Terra Nova* in new pancake ice, 1912. *[A108/001277; SP4585]*

Iceberg passed on voyage home, 1912. *[A108/001279; SP4587]*

Iceberg passed on voyage home, 1912. *[A108/001280; SP4588]*

Sledger at the foot of glacier and Mt. Erebus, 1912. *[A108/001285; SP4593]*

Christmas Eve in the pack, December, 1912. *[A108/001301; SP4609]*

Mt. Erebus at midnight from *Terra Nova* off Cape Bird, January 3, 1911. *[A108/001304; SP4612]*

Cloud effect. Ross Sea, January 2, 1911. *[A108/001305; SP4613]*

Mt. Erebus at midnight from the *Terra Nova* off Cape Bird, January 3, 1911. *[A108/001306; SP4614]*

The ice foot looking to Cape Royds from *Terra Nova*, January 1911. *[A108/001308; SP4616]*

Looking to Cape Barne from Cape Evans: mirage effect, March 3, 1911. *[A108/001317; SP4625]*

Iceberg off Cape Evans, March 1911. *[A108/001319; SP4627]*

Looking to Cape Barne from Cape Evans: mirage effect, March 3, 1911. *[A108/001320; SP4628]*

Cloud effect, North Bay and Barne Glacier, March 26, 1911. *[A108/001322; SP4630]*

Cloud effect in the Sound, March 26, 1911. *[A108/001324; SP4632]*

First appearance of the Sun over Barne Glacier, August 26, 1911. *[A108/001331; SP4639]*

Cloud effect on ice. Cape Royds, November 27, 1911. *[A108/001362; SP4670]*

Cloud effect on ice. Cape Royds, November 1911. *[A108/001363; SP4671]*

Frost smoke off Glacier Tongue, 1910–1912. *[A108/001494; SP4802]*

Frost smoke off Glacier Tongue, 1910–1912. *[A108/001497; SP4805]*

Sunset. Antarctic Ocean with gull, 1910–1912. *[A108/001515; SP4823]*

Royal Geographical Society's Herbert Ponting *Terra Nova* photographs that appear in With Scott to the Pole:

Page 2: The Matterhorn Berg, profile, and Mt. Erebus (Clissold on summit), October 8, 1911. *[A108/001073; SP4381]*

Page 3 and jacket: Herbert Ponting and telephoto apparatus, January 1912. *[A108/001236; SP4544]*

Pages 4–5: Mt. Erebus and ice reflection in foreground, January 7, 1911. *[A108/000838; SP4146]*

Page 7: Evening in the pack. Christmas Eve, December 24, 1910. *[A108/000772; SP4080]*

Page 25: Group of all the shore party (except Clissold, laid up and Ponting, photographing). Taken outside the hut, October 1911. *[A108/001101; SP4409]*

Page 26: Captain Oates and ponies in stable, May 26, 1911. *[A108/001009; SP4317]*

Page 27: From the top of the Aft deck house of *Terra Nova*. Pancake floe after entering the pack, December 9, 1910. *[A108/000748; SP4056]*

Page 29: Furling *Terra Nova's* mainsail in the pack, December 1910. *[A108/001302; SP4610]*

Page 30: Cinematographing *Terra Nova's* bow forcing aside the floes, December 1910. *[A108/001297; SP4605]*

Page 31: *Terra Nova* held up in the pack, December 13, 1910. *[A108/000759; SP4066]*

Page 32: Lieutenant Rennick leading one of the ponies on to the sea ice, January 1911. *[A108/001311; SP4619]*

Page 33: Hut, bergs, and clouds, December 1911. *[A108/001176; SP4484]*

Page 37: Captain Scott and group taken on the return of the Southern Party, April 13, 1911. *[A108/000980; SP4288]*

Page 39 (top): Nelson's "lab" and Nelson at work, March 30, 1911. *[A108/000977; SP4285]*

Page 39 (bottom): Meares at the pianola, January 1912. *[A108/001224; SP4532]*

Page 40: Doctor Wilson, Lieutenant Bowers, and Cherry-Garrard before leaving for Cape Crozier, June 27, 1911. *[A108/001030; SP4338]*

Page 41: Doctor Wilson, Lieutenant Bowers, and Cherry-Garrard on the return from their winter trip to Cape Crozier, August 1, 1911. *[A108/001038; SP4346]*

Page 43: Captain Scott and Southern Party. Mt. Erebus in background, January 26, 1911. *[A108/000884; SP4192]*

Pages 52 (inset) and 122: Captain Scott, April 13, 1911. *[A108/000981; SP4289]*

Pages 69 and 88: Ponting biographing (photographing) "Watering Ship," December 11, 1910. *[A108/000754; SP4062]*

Page 70: View of the deck of *Terra Nova* with dogs from Engine Room hatch, January 3, 1911. *[A108/000805; SP4113]*

Page 71: Captain Oates and some of the ponies, 1910–1912. *[A108/000785; SP4093]*

Page 72: Portrait of Wilfred Bruce on *Terra Nova*, 1910–1912. *[A108/001496; SP4804]*

Page 73: Lieutenant Rennick on *Terra Nova*, 1910–1912. *[A108/001503; SP4811]*

Page 74: A warm day in the pack (crew asleep on deck), December 1910. *[A108/001294; SP4602]*

Page 75: At the pump. *Terra Nova*, December 1910. *[A108/001293; SP4601]*

Page 76: Oxo for the man at the wheel, 1910–1912. *[A108/001516; SP4824]*

Page 77: At the pumps in a gale in the Antarctic Ocean, March 1912. *[A108/001509; SP4817]*

Page 78: Entering the pack. Fo'c'sle of *Terra Nova*, December 9, 1910. *[A108/000747; SP4055]*

Page 79: Evening sky effect in pack, December 9, 1910. *[A108/000750; SP4058]*

Page 80: In the ice pack from the main top of *Terra Nova* (Gran, Taylor, and Wright), December 22, 1910. *[A108/000782; SP4090]*

Page 81: In the ice pack from the main top of *Terra Nova* (T. Gran and Lees), December 12, 1910. *[A108/000783; SP4091]*

Page 84 (top): Letting down the water bottle from *Terra Nova*, December 17, 1910. *[A108/000788; SP4096]*

Page 84 (bottom): Doctor Wilson shooting from *Terra Nova*, 1910–1912. *[A108/000789; SP4097]*

Page 85: Group in Wardroom of *Terra Nova*, 1910–1912. *[A108/000790; SP4098]*

Page 86: *Terra Nova* held up in the pack. Ice bollard in the foreground, December 13, 1910. *[A108/000780; SP4068]*

Page 87: Anchored to the ice, December 11, 1910. *[A108/000752; SP4060]*

Page 89: Nelson and Priestley making a hole in a floe. Debenham watching, December 1910. *[A108/001286; SP4594]*

Page 90: Christmas Eve in the pack, December 1912. *[A108/001300; SP4608]*

Page 91: Working the pram (boat) through pack to get at penguins, December 1910. *[A108/001288; SP4596]*

Page 92: Telephoto. Berg in pack. Gran and McLeod on ice, December 20, 1910. *[A108/000769; SP4077]*

Page 93: Light effect on pack, December 22, 1910. *[A108/000770; SP4078]*

Page 94: Mt. Erebus at 11:00 p.m., January 3, 1911. *[A108/000820; SP4128]*

Page 95: Back Door Bay. Cape Royds showing sharp line of shadow on Mt. Erebus, February 16, 1911. *[A108/000920; SP4228]*

Page 98: Grotto in a berg. *Terra Nova* in distance. Taylor and Wright (interior), January 5, 1911. *[A108/000825; SP4133]*

Page 99: A berg with a large grotto, January 5, 1911. *[A108/000826; SP4134]*

Page 100 (top): Mt. Erebus with Adélie penguins on ice in foreground and open water near the grotto berg, January 5, 1911. *[A108/000827; SP4135]*

Page 100 (bottom): Skua chick and eggs found in same nest. Chick about one week (with rule for comparison), January 6, 1911. *[A108/000831; SP4139]*

Page 101: Ponting cinematographing skua gulls, January 7, 1911. *[A108/000847; SP4155]*

Page 102: Beautiful broken ice, reflections, and *Terra Nova*, January 7, 1911. *[A108/000844; SP4152]*

Page 103: Captain Scott, Wilson, and Evans returning to the ship across the ice, January 9, 1911. *[A108/000851; SP4159]*

Page 104: Officers hauling sledges of fodder from *Terra Nova* to Cape Evans, January 1911. *[A108/001313; SP4621]*

Page 105: Getting the ill-fated motor sledge off the ship, January 8, 1911. *[A108/000849; SP4157]*

Page 106: Lunch in the tent, January 7, 1911. *[A108/000848; SP4156]*

Page 107 (top): Davies, the carpenter, working on hut, January 10, 1911. *[A108/000854; SP4162]*

Page 107 (bottom): Forde and Abbott building hut, January 10, 1911. *[A108/000855; SP4163]*

Page 108: *Terra Nova* at ice foot, Cape Barne, and glacier in background, January 15, 1911. *[A108/000869; SP4177]*

Page 109: Smoke cloud from Mt. Erebus, January 15, 1911. *[A108/000865; SP4173]*

Page 110: Doctor Simpson taking observations on Vane Hill, March 1911. *[A108/001327; SP4635]*

Page 111: The waning daylight. Sun over the Barne Glacier at midday, March 26, 1911. *[A108/001323; SP4631]*

Page 112: Getting the camp in order. Mt. Erebus (and Colman's), January 23, 1911. *[A108/000878; SP4186]*

Page 113 (top): Laying a depot. H & P's biscuits, February 8, 1911. *[A108/000889; SP4197]*

Page 113 (bottom): Sledge party having Colman's corn flour, February 7, 1911. *[A108/000887; SP4195]*

Page 114 (top): Giving whisky to a pony that swam ashore, February 8, 1911. *[A108/000893; SP4201]*

Page 114 (bottom): Giving whisky to a pony that swam ashore, February 8, 1911. *[A108/000892; SP4200]*

Page 115 and jacket: Steward Hooper eating baked beans on a wooden box advertising Heinz, 1910–1912. *[A108/001423; SP4731]*

Page 118: H. G. Ponting and cinematograph, 1910–1912. *[A108/001235; SP4543]*

Page 119: *Terra Nova* and a berg at ice foot, January 16, 1911. *[A108/000872; SP4180]*

Page 120 (top left): Portrait of B. Day on his return from the Barrier, December 21, 1911. *[A108/001184; SP4492]*

Page 120 (top middle): Portrait of Hooper on his return from the Barrier, December 21, 1911. *[A108/001185; SP4493]*

Page 120 (top right): Portrait of Demetri after his return from the Barrier, January 1912. *[A108/001206; SP4514]*

Page 120 (bottom left): Portrait of C. H. Meares after his return from the Barrier, January 1912. *[A108/001207; SP4515]*

Page 120 (bottom middle): P. Keohane on his return from the Barrier, January 1912. *[A108/001241; SP4549]*

Page 120 (bottom right): Cherry-Garrard on his return from the Barrier, January 29, 1912. *[A108/001231; SP4539]*

Page 121: C. S. Wright on his return from the Barrier, January 29, 1912. *[A108/001232; SP4540]*

Page 123 (top left): Dr. E. A. Wilson, April 21, 1911. *[A108/000990; SP4298]*

Page 123 (top right): C. S. Wright, April 13, 1911. *[A108/000986; SP4294]*

Page 123 (bottom left): Lieutenant Evans, April 13, 1911. *[A108/000982; SP4290]*

Page 123 (bottom right): T. Gran, April 13, 1911. *[A108/000987; SP4295]*

Page 124: Griffith Taylor, April 13, 1911. *[A108/000985; SP4293]*

Page 125: Evans and Crean, April 13, 1911. *[A108/000988; SP4296]*

Pages 126–127 and 217: Telephoto of Mt. Lister, February 10, 1911. *[A108/000902; SP4210]*

Page 128: Wave at West Beach, February 28, 1911. *[A108/000932; SP4240]*

Page 129: Wave breaking at West Beach, February 28, 1911. *[A108/000933; SP4241]*

Page 130 (top left): Sastrugi on Barne Glacier, February 21, 1911. *[A108/000930; SP4238]*

Page 130 (top right): Heavy pancake ice (several feet thick in layers) in which the ship was held whilst trying to rescue the Northern Party, 1912. *[A108/001265; SP4573]*

Page 130 (bottom left): Young ice forming. North wind. North Bay, 2:40 p.m., March 7, 1911. *[A108/000947; SP4255]*

Page 130 (bottom right): Weathered ice furrows after a blizzard at Cape Evans, March 8, 1911. *[A108/000952; SP4260]*

Page 131: Pancake ice forming into floe off Cape Evans, March 15, 1911. *[A108/000961; SP4269]*

Page 132: A view of Hut Point, November 4, 1911. *[A108/001113; SP4421]*

Pages 132–133: Mt. Erebus and dome cloud from West Beach, 2:30 p.m., icicled glacier in foreground, March 7, 1911. *[A108/000941; SP4249]*

Page 134: Ice cave in Land's End Glacier. Captain Scott, April 28, 1911. *[A108/000996; SP4304]*

Page 135: Caves in Land's End Glacier, April 28, 1911. *[A108/000993; SP4301]*

Page 138: Hut and Mt. Erebus photographed by moonlight, June 13, 1911. *[A108/001025; SP4333]*

Page 139: Lieutenant Evans observing an occultation of Jupiter, June 8, 1911. *[A108/001022; SP4330]*

Page 140: In the stable, May 25, 1911. *[A108/001008; SP4316]*

Pages 141 and 219 (top): Meares and Oates at the blubber stove, May 26, 1911. *[A108/001010; SP4318]*

Page 142: Evans and Crean mending sleeping bags, May 16, 1911. *[A108/001000; SP4308]*

Page 143 (top): Taylor and Debenham in cubicle, May 22, 1911. *[A108/001005; SP4313]*

Page 143 (bottom): Lieutenant Evans draughting, May 23, 1911. *[A108/001006; SP4314]*

Page 144: Clissold the cook at the galley, August 30, 1911. *[A108/001045; SP4354]*

Page 145: Clissold the cook making bread, March 26, 1911. *[A108/000974; SP4282]*

Page 146: E. W. Nelson testing thermometers, July 14, 1911. *[A108/001035; SP4343]*

Page 147: Doctor Atkinson in his lab, September 15, 1911. *[A108/001052; SP4360]*

Page 148: Doctor Atkinson, Bowers, and Cherry-Garrard cutting up pemmican, June 23, 1911. *[A108/001028; SP4335]*

Page 149: Captain Scott's birthday dinner, June 6, 1911. *[A108/001019; SP4327]*

Page 150: F. Debenham grinding geological specimens, July 12, 1911. *[A108/001033; SP4341]*

Page 151: Doctor Simpson at the telephone and sidereal clock, July 14, 1911. *[A108/001034; SP4342]*

Page 152: Cherry-Garrard working on the *South Polar Times*, August 30, 1911. *[A108/001043; SP4351]*

Page 153: Keohane finishing his model of *Terra Nova*, August 10, 1911. *[A108/001041; SP4349]*

Page 154: Petty Officer Evans at the sewing machine overhauling sleeping bags and tents, 1910–1912. *[A108/001251; SP4559]*

Page 155: Doctor Simpson at work in the magnetic hut, January 5, 1912. *[A108/001202; SP4509]*

Page 156: The tenements—bunks in the hut of Bowers, Cherry-Garrard, Oates, Meares, and Atkinson, October 9, 1911. *[A108/001077; SP4385]*

Page 157: Herbert Ponting lecturing on Japan using lantern slides, October 16, 1911. *[A108/001078; SP4386]*

Page 158: Captain Scott writing in his journal in his den, October 7, 1911. *[A108/001066; SP4374]*

Page 159: Sledges laid out, hut, glacier, and cloud effect, December 19, 1911. *[A108/001177; SP4485]*

Page 162: The pressure ridges of the ice crack from the Barne Glacier to Inaccessible Island looking to Cape Royds (Captain Scott), October 8, 1911. *[A108/001069; SP4377]*

Page 163: Curiously weathered (or sea-washed) berg in South Bay with Mt. Erebus, October 8, 1911. *[A108/001071; SP4379]*

Page 164 (top): F. Debenham and plane table, September 9, 1911. *[A108/001047; SP4355]*

Page 164 (bottom): F. Debenham making a plane table survey, September 9, 1911. *[A108/001049; SP4357]*

Page 165: Huge ice bastions of the Castle Berg (Clissold at base), September 17, 1911. *[A108/001056; SP4364]*

Page 166: The Castle Berg with dog sledge, September 17, 1911. *[A108/001053; SP4361]*

Page 167: Castle Berg. Flashlight, June 4, 1911. *[A108/001018; SP4326]*

Page 170 (top): Day's motor and load passing Inaccessible Island, November 1911. *[A108/001359; SP4667]*

Page 170 (bottom): Lieutenant Evans guiding Day's motor past the bergs, November 1911. *[A108/001360; SP4668]*

Page 171 and jacket: Western party crossing the ice to the ship, March 1911. *[A108/001521; SP4829]*

Page 172: Lieut. T. Gran on skis in rough ice, October 1911. *[A108/001105; SP4413]*

Page 173: Ponting cooling his head, January 1912. *[A108/001243; SP4551]*

Page 174: Nelson's igloo and Mt. Erebus, December 24, 1911. *[A108/001187; SP4495]*

Page 175 (top): Nelson and his winch (winding), December 24, 1911. *[A108/001193; SP4501]*

Page 175 (bottom): Nelson's winch on sledge, December 24, 1911. *[A108/001194; SP4502]*

Page 176: Doctor Wilson and pony Nobby rolling, October 1911. *[A108/001082; SP4390]*

Page 177: Mr. Cherry-Garrard and pony Michael rolling, October 1911. *[A108/001084; SP4392]*

Page 178: Clissold, Anton, and an Emperor penguin, 1910–1912. *[A108/001487; SP4795]*

Page 179: The penguinery. Cape Royds and Mt. Erebus, November 27, 1911. *[A108/001154; SP4462]*

Page 180 (top): Weddell seal at West Beach, 1910–1912. *[A108/001476; SP4784]*

Page 180 (bottom): Seal in a hole, 1910–1912. *[A108/001491; SP4799]*

Page 181: Skuas and a dead penguin with ponies behind, 1910–1912. *[A108/001483; SP4791]*

Page 184 (top left): Husky Kasoi, 1910–1912. *[A108/001433; SP4741]*

Page 184 (top right): Husky Trésor, 1910–1912. *[A108/001436; SP4744]*

Page 184 (bottom left): Husky Ostrenos, 1910–1912. *[A108/001453; SP4761]*

Page 184 (bottom right): Husky Mannike Noogis, 1910–1912. *[A108/001438; SP4746]*

Page 185 (top left): Husky Biela Noogis, 1910–1912. *[A108/001455; SP4763]*

Page 185 (top right): Husky Cook, 1910–1912. *[A108/001456; SP4764]*

Page 185 (bottom left): Husky Vaida, 1910–1912. *[A108/001446; SP4754]*

Page 185 (bottom right): Husky Osman, 1910–1912. *[A108/001464; SP4772]*

Page 186 (top left): Husky Chris, 1910–1912. *[A108/001458; SP4766]*

Page 186 (top right): Husky Bieleglas, 1910–1912. *[A108/001454; SP4762]*

Page 186 (bottom): Husky Stareek, 1910–1912. *[A108/001447; SP4755]*

Page 187: Weddell seals basking on the floes, 1910–1912. *[A108/001469; SP4777]*

Page 188: Seals lying by Church Berg, December 29, 1911. *[A108/001453; SP4761]*

Page 189: Part of Church Berg showing grotto, December 29, 1911. *[A108/001200; SP4508]*

Page 190: Cloud effect on the ice, Cape Royds, November 27, 1911. *[A108/001150; SP4458]*

Page 191: Cape Barne, November 29, 1911. *[A108/001148; SP4456]*

Page 194 (top): *Terra Nova* at Butter Point for Western Party, 1912. *[A108/001268; SP4576]*

Page 194 (bottom): Passing a large tabular berg, 1912. *[A108/001281; SP4589]*

Page 195: Lillie with a large glass sponge, 1912. *[A108/001271; SP4579]*

Page 196: Group of crew of *Terra Nova*, 1912. *[A108/001283; SP4591]*

Page 197: View of crow's nest of *Terra Nova*, 1910–1912. *[A108/001524; SP4832]*

Page 198: Dealing out Fry's chocolate on *Terra Nova*, 1910–1912. *[A108/001518; SP4826]*

Page 199: *Terra Nova* in heavy weather, 1912. *[A108/001284; SP4592]*

Page 200: End of the Barrier at Cape Crozier, January 3, 1911. *[A108/000811; SP4119]*

Page 201: Herbert Ponting cinematographing whales, 1910–1912. *[A108/001539; SP4847]*

Page 203: Portrait of Herbert Ponting on *Terra Nova*, 1910–1912. *[A108/001498; SP4806]*

Page 210: Herbert Ponting at work in the darkroom, July 22, 1911. *[A108/001037; SP4345]*

Page 212: Ponting photographing ship, *Terra Nova* in pack, December 1910. *[A108/001501; SP4809]*

Page 213 (bottom): Ponting at work in his darkroom, March 24, 1911. *[A108/000967; SP4275]*

Page 214: *Terra Nova* in a gale, March 1912. *[A108/001508; SP4816]*

Page 219 (bottom): Portrait of C. H. Meares after his return from the Barrier, January 1912. *[A108/001208; SP4516]*

Page 221: West from Barne Glacier to Cape Barne, February 21, 1911. *[A108/000925; SP4233]*

Page 225 (inset): Nelson's old hole snowed up. He is pointing at the old hole, December 24, 1911. *[A108/001195; SP4503]*

Scott Polar Research Institute's Herbert Ponting *Terra Nova* photographs that appear in With Scott to the Pole:

Pages 8–9, 22–23, 54–55, 68–69, 202–203, 224–225: The first stage: the men unload *Terra Nova* near Cape Evans, 1910–1912. *[82_11_10]*

Pages 34–35: *Terra Nova* with iceberg and men in foreground, 1910–1912. *[82_11_24]*

Pages 82–83: Ice landscape with penguins, 1910–1912. *[82_11_35]*

Pages 96–97, 240, and endpaper: Ice landscape, 1910–1912. *[82_11_06]*

Pages 116–117: *Terra Nova* tied to the ice foot with berg in foreground, 1910–1912. *[82_11_17]*

Pages 136–137: Cape Evans and depots of supplies, 1910–1912. *[82_11_41]*

Pages 160–161: Man-hauling, 1910–1912. *[82_11_22]*

Pages 168–169: Preparation for the Southern Journey, 1910–1912. *[82_11]*

Pages 182–183: Hooper and Demetri on the ice with seals, 1910–1912. *[82_11_23]*

Pages 192–193: Men with boat and ship in background, 1910–1912. *[82_11_07]*

Endpaper: Ice landscape, 1910–1912. *[82_11_36]*

Picture Acknowledgments

The majority of the photographs in this book are from the Royal Geographical Society and Scott Polar Research Institute archives. Most of these photographs are listed at the end of the Gallery section (pages 239–240). Other Royal Geographical Society and Scott Polar Research Institute pictures are listed below.

Royal Geographical Society pictures are found on pages:
9 (inset), 12, 13, 14 (top), 14 (bottom), 15, 16, 17, 18 (top), 18 (bottom), 19, 20, 21 (top), 21 (bottom), 36, 44, 45, 58 (inset), 58 (main picture), and 60

Scott Polar Research Institute pictures are found on pages:
11, 23, 42, 47, 49, 50, 51, 52 (main picture), 53, 55 (inset), 56, 57, 59, 61, 62, 63, 64–65, 66, and 67

In addition, the following pictures appear in this book.

Page 204
Portrait of Herbert Ponting as a young man
Courtesy of H. J. P. Arnold

Page 205
Ships in San Francisco Bay
Courtesy of H. J. P. Arnold

Page 206 (top left)
At the crater's brink, Asama-Yama
From *In Lotus-Land: Japan*, 1910

Page 206 (top right)
Smoke and steam rising from Asama's crater after the explosion
From *In Lotus-Land: Japan*, 1910

Page 207
Photographing at the crater's lip, Aso-San
From *In Lotus-Land: Japan*, 1910

Page 208
Sunset on Mount Fuji
From *In Lotus-Land: Japan*, 1910

Page 209
Cover of In Lotus Land: Japan
From *In Lotus-Land: Japan*, 1910

Page 211 (top)
The "Ponco" Unburstable Inner Tube
Courtesy of H. J. P. Arnold

Page 211 (bottom)
Charlie Chaplin
Courtesy of H. J. P. Arnold

Page 213 (top)
Newman Sinclair cine camera advertisement
Courtesy of H. J. P. Arnold

Page 215 (top)
Ponting being attacked by Killer whales
From *The Great White South*, 1921

Page 215 (bottom)
Ponting posing with camera
Courtesy of H. J. P. Arnold

Page 218
Terra Nova photographed from the ice grotto
Courtesy of Seventh Continent Trust

Page 222
The aurora
Courtesy of Popperfoto.com